Photography by Ray Main

# suzanne davy

# 101 IDEAS
## bedrooms

quadrille

Editorial Director  Jane O'Shea
Art Director  Helen Lewis
Designer  Paul Welti
Project Editor  Hilary Mandleberg
Production  Beverley Richardson

Photography  Ray Main

First published in 2004 by
Quadrille Publishing Limited
Alhambra House
27–31 Charing Cross Road
London WC2H 0LS

This paperback edition first published in 2005
10 9 8 7 6 5 4 3 2

British Library Cataloguing-in-Publication
Data. A catalogue record for this book is
available from the British Library.

ISBN 1 84400 153 9

Every effort has been made to ensure the
accuracy of the information in this book. In no
circumstances can the publisher or the author
accept any liability for any loss, injury or
damage of any kind resulting from any error in
or omission from the information contained in
this book.

Printed and bound in China

# contents

## part one
## the big picture

# part one

# the big picture

# where do I start?
## five things to do before you begin

Designing your bedroom should be a creative and satisfying business, but to keep the project on track, a degree of practicality is essential as a starting point.

## jottings

Small practical procedures will make a big difference to your organisational process! Arm yourself with a pen and notebook because you'll find inspiration all around you and will need to jot down sources, references and ideas.

## money, measure and management

You'll find a calculator, long tape measure and colour-coded files or folders essential. Shoe boxes might come in handy for storing inspirational finds. Also, tags, tape, light glue, paper clips and pins.

## inspirational stuff

Be like a squirrel and hoard magazines, brochures and colour charts. The back pages of interior design magazines are a rich source for manufacturers' brochures. At this stage just have fun exploring your intuitive awareness of styles, colours and shapes.

## stripping

Thinking about how your bedroom will look naked will help you make a critical appraisal; you'll find that the room's architecture, natural light and spatial potential will be revealed (see 3). An undressed bedroom may also suggest a more thorough decorating programme than you had envisaged!

## questions, questions

Write down questions as and when they arise. You don't have to answer them all yet, but they will help your scheme evolve. Your list of questions – and answers – will grow as your plan develops. For example, are there any basic priorities such as re-wiring and plumbing? Do I have to compromise with existing decorations and furnishings? Where do I go for inspiration?

# 2 make a wish list

A wish list is a useful exercise to help you prioritise what you want to achieve in your bedroom. Obviously, if there are two of you, it's essential to explore and express your individual likes and dislikes – and probably find compromise on the way!

## overall benefits
- I want a bedroom that will add to the value of my house
- I want to maximise the space
- I want a quick, cheap update
- I want to get away from street noise and pollution

## function
- I want a sexy bedroom
- I want a quiet haven that I can retreat to
- I want a room where I can work sometimes
- I want a room where I can listen to my music
- I want a room where I can bathe
- I want a room to put up a guest
- I want somewhere to display my picture collection

## fittings and fixtures
- I need generous cupboard space
- I want a hideaway office
- I need masses of bookshelves
- I want a way to zone the bed area

## details
- I want a hardwood floor
- I want to include under-floor heating
- I want a huge modern bed
- I want better lighting and heating

# what are my assets? 3

Every bedroom has potential, however forlorn it might appear at the outset, so find ways of highlighting its merits.

## space

• Create an en-suite bathroom or an in-room bathing area
• Increase your storage or cupboard space
• Buy a new big bed
• In a high-ceilinged room, take advantage and install a mezzanine or bed platform

## good natural light

• Make the most of it: don't block it with heavy curtains
• Choose colours to maximise its effect

## architectural detail

• Mouldings, period windows, old fireplaces and panelled doors all add character and decorating potential

## floor

• Old floorboards don't have to be covered (see 71)
• A carpet in good condition will free up a lot of your budget

## furniture and ornament

• If you already have good storage space, lucky you!
• A special piece of furniture you possess may influence your decorative direction
• A dynamic painting or picture can be the starting point for your colour theme (see 96).

# dump the no-hopers 4

Now is the time to take stock. Update or renovate where you can, but don't jeopardise your new bedroom by hanging on to things.

## flooring

Flooring is not the place to compromise (see 71-96). If an old carpet is beyond hope, or is highly coloured or patterned, get rid of it rather than ruin the harmony of your new scheme.

## bedroom furniture

If your bed has started to sag or squeak, it's time to buy a new one (see 78–80). This is also the moment to get rid of cheaply made built-in furniture and go for some updated storage instead (see 85).

## wires and pipes

There will never be a better opportunity to get rid of visible pipework and dangling electric wires.

## lighting

If all you have is a central ceiling light in your bedroom, it's likely that it'll only provide unflattering illumination. If you can, replace it with downlights, wall and table lamps; if you can't, a dimmer switch might help (see 53–56).

# top tips for tiny bedrooms 5

Making the most of a tiny space involves crafty use of space, colour, lighting and furnishings.

## shape and line

Keep the decorative scheme simple and make the bed the focus, preferably positioned opposite the door to draw the eye. An oversize object such as a very large picture behind the bed can give the illusion of space. Vertical or horizontal lines or stripes visually accentuate height or length respectively but dominating pattern or shape elsewhere will counteract the effect.

## colour

Cool colours such as light greens and blues recede, so creating a sense of space. A hint of yellow in the green and red in the blue helps to avoid a 'cold' atmosphere while using a darker 'anchor' colour prevents pale colours looking insipid and gives definition. A ceiling in a pale, neutral colour – preferably not pure white – with a slight sheen will reflect and enhance natural light.

## lighting

An uncluttered window maximises natural light – choose blinds or shutters rather than curtains. Balanced electric lighting around the room prevents shadowy corners and walls can be 'extended' with uplights. Slender, elongated lamps and shades accentuate height while wall- or bed-mounted reading lights save space. Take care when using spotlights as they are inclined to create harsh pools of light and upset the decorative rhythm.

## mirrors

Mirrors maximise light but a large area of them can create glare and be unnerving. Instead, use mirror in panels – for example on the front of cupboard doors or either side of the bed.

## furniture and storage

Small furniture won't make the room look bigger; it's better to have fewer good-sized pieces. Dual-purpose storage saves space: a bed with drawers underneath, a window seat, a blanket box bedside table, even a fold-down 'vanity' table in a cupboard to keep clutter to a minimum. If possible, have sliding doors on cupboards and replace protruding handles with flush ones or touch-opening magnets as appropriate.

# under the eaves

There's something very appealing about sleeping under the eaves, but only when there's enough room to stand up straight when you get out of bed! The inherent quirkiness of the space lends it great character and this can be exploited to create a uniquely attractive environment. But any conversion will require the expertise of an architect, surveyor or builder who will offer guidance on building regulations, structural requirements and planning permission.

## fitting furniture

Furniture needs to be low and streamlined but this means problematic clothes storage. You could build a false wall 'hung' from the ceiling but this will upset the symmetry of the space. A more radical solution is a freestanding cupboard and drawer unit. One side gives access to your clothes and the other can be your 'headboard'.

## bed placement

The bed has to be positioned so you don't hit your head every time you sit up. Apart from the freestanding unit option, the obvious solution is to put the bed against the gable wall, though if there's a window in it you may not have room for a bedhead. In this case, have an oversized headboard and turn the bed round to face the window.

## making it special

There is little opportunity in an attic bedroom to use fabrics, wallcoverings, pictures and ornamentation, so focus on the room's interesting lines and features instead. If there's a lot of floor, exploit it with a wood or laminate floor. With low ceilings, clever lighting – floor lighting, for example – can help avoid any sense of claustrophobia and if there's plenty of space, think about incorporating a toilet and shower behind a false wall.

## advantages of creating a loft bedroom

- Adds value to the house
- Makes use of wasted space
- Appealing character
- Removed from the main hubbub of the house
- The space can be larger than any other room in the house
- The views may be great

## disadvantages of creating a loft bedroom

- Cost
- Intrusiveness of access stairs
- Difficult to get correct balance of light and heat
- Arrangement of furniture can be awkward
- Difficult access for large furniture
- Loss of storage space

# 7 children's rooms

A child's room needs to grow with the child. Starting off as a quiet, warm place for baby to sleep, it's not long before it becomes a playground, study area, sports hall, den and karaoke club.

## space-saving sleeping

At the toddler stage, a bed built into a wall unit or a low platform bed are good choices. A more dramatic option is to construct a low mezzanine with the bed up a short flight of stairs and a study and play area beneath.

## furniture

Avoid purpose-made kids' furniture and stick instead to a good shelving system and adaptable furniture. A couple of low chests of drawers with laminated board on top offer storage space, a hideaway den and, later, a desk.

## storage

Use colour-coded boxes or baskets for larger toys and hanging drawstring bags for smaller items. Store books in a basket or on a low shelf, but keep special books on higher shelves out of the reach of sticky fingers.

## windows

Windows must have safety catches and/or locks that can be opened easily in case of fire.

## flooring

Go for easy-care flooring like rubber floorboards or laminate (see 66, 67), but for the crawling and learning-to-walk stage, a large area rug will make life's ups and downs easier.

## lighting

All electrical sockets must be childproof. For children who are afraid of the dark, dimmer switches and low-wattage skirting fixtures are discreet. Older children need task lighting for study, hobbies and reading in bed.

## decoration

A child's tastes and interests change so use easy-to-alter paint rather than wallpaper. Other details such as curtains, bed linen, lampshades and cushions can be updated without too much trouble and expense.

# 8 do I need a professional?

If your bedroom and en-suite bathroom project involves work that you can't undertake yourself you will need some professional input. This list will help you identify the sort of people you may have to call on and explains what they do.

## architect
- Converts your ideas into reality
- Provides working drawings; deals with planning applications
- Period conservation and restoration
- Construction techniques
- Project management
- Special requirements, such as air-conditioning and en-suite bathroom design

## lighting consultant
- Specialist in lighting design using the latest technology and effects

## builder
- Renovation
- Removing or constructing partition walls
- Stripping walls, plastering and finishing
- Installing doors and windows
- General electrics and plumbing
- Hard flooring and general carpentry
- General painting and decorating, and tiling

## joiner
- Built-in cupboards and complex shelving
- Bed platforms
- Pelmet and headboard cut-outs
- Window frame and door resizing and hanging
- Renovation of wooden floors

## plumber
- Bathroom and toilet installation
- Water and heating expertise

## electrician
- Advice on wiring safety compliance
- Planning and installation of sockets, switches, and lighting
- Re-wiring

## interior designer
- Stylistic guidance
- Descriptive drawings
- Access to a wide range of samples
- Advice on lighting and ornamentation

- A link between architect and client
- Knowledge of special finishes, paint effects, carpets, fabrics and materials

## upholsterer, curtain maker and soft furnisher

- Bedhead and bed hangings
- Made-to-order bolsters and cushions
- Loose or fitted chair and sofa covers
- Making and hanging curtains and blinds

# 9 set a budget

First decide whether you are going to pay for the work out of pocket, stagger the work and the payment, or borrow to fund your bedroom makeover. Once you've decided how much you are able to spend, put aside 10% of the total for the inevitable unforeseen contingencies. Keep in mind that your outlay will relate to whether you want to add capital value to the property or whether you are just doing an economic makeover. You will need to allocate your budget proportionally, depending on the relative expense of each part of the work. For example:

- General building costs
- New en suite
- Re-wiring
- Painting and decorating
- Flooring, fixtures and fittings including bed and joinery
- Fabrics and making-up costs
- Professional fees (see 10)

If you go over your budget, don't panic (see 11).

# 10 cost it out

Make three lists to help you draw up your budget. The first sets out the major works, to include structural alterations, electrics and plumbing, en-suite bathroom upgrading or installation, joinery and flooring. Don't forget to budget for any professional help.

The second list costs out wallpaper and papering, paint and painting, bed, fabric, furniture, window treatment, storage, light fittings, audio and TV system. Again, factor in professional help with these components.

The third list includes all the accessories that you have to buy new (well, retail therapy is vital!) such as bed linen, pillows, cushions, throws, rugs, mirrors and decorative objects.

Try to be realistic about what you can afford, remembering to keep 10% for contingencies. Always keep necessity, quality and comfort in mind when you define your priorities!

# 11
# small budget – big ideas five ways to make your money go further

For the 'where's my cake, I want to eat it' moment your options are DIY, phasing the work or exploring some cost-cutting ideas.

### 1 • doing your own thing

Your three-part list (see 10) will help you identify which sections of your bedroom project you can tackle yourself. Don't be over-ambitious though because you will waste time, energy and, ultimately, money. However, doing all the painting and wallpapering, and painting any newly made storage furniture, for example, will save you a lot of money.

### 2 • phasing the work

See if your budget will cover your absolute priorities such as rewiring and plumbing, a new bed or an en-suite shower, for example. Another option is to install the plumbing up to first fit, in other words, putting in the pipework only and installing the fittings at a later date when you have more funds.

### 3 • paint it on

Paint is less expensive than wallpaper and painting saves time and effort as well. It's also more versatile because of its range of colours and finishes and, if you make a bad choice, you can always have another go.

### 4 • material world

You can save money on fabrics by using cheaper materials but in generous quantities for curtains and bed dressing: dress silk instead of silk taffeta, muslin rather than voile, cotton replacing linen. Instead of curtains, you might like to make a feature out of a home-painted blind.

### 5 • feature focus

Go for chic minimalism with maximum effect by making a stunning feature of one piece of furniture – probably the bed – and focus maximum attention on that area. This will set the tone for your high standards and the future direction of the scheme when money allows.

# 12

# bedroom upgrade

Instead of going for a complete refit, it's easy enough to change the look of your bedroom by concentrating on one or two major features, or by going for some quick decorative fixes.

## three major options

**1 • Floor:** as flooring is crucial, a new-look floor will go a long way to rejuvenating the room. To upgrade the existing floorboards, sand, fill and finish them appropriately or, if they can't be satisfactorily renovated, you might paint a broad border around the perimeter and cover the rest of the floor with a large rug. If this process is too laborious, a new carpet may be preferable!

**2 • Window:** if you have only had blinds before, adding curtains will change the visual emphasis of the bedroom. Professionally made curtains add substance and drama to a scheme.

**3 • Bed:** expense, rather than time and effort, will get you a luxury new bed in a style that could suggest a new decorative direction for you to follow.

## five quick fixes

**1 • Walls:** colour refreshes the decorative emphasis and paint is the easiest and cheapest way to achieve this. Alternatively, change the look from plain to patterned with a wallpaper or, for a fresh and opulent look, line the entire wall behind the bed with a fabric such as felt or damask.

**2 • Ceiling:** painting the ceiling a contrast colour will change the room's visual dynamic.

**3 • Window:** replace a dated window treatment with a simple modern blind, shutters or sheer curtain. If you have treasured curtains, give them new life with a broad fabric border.

**4 • Bed:** new bed dressing will immediately refresh your bedroom look. Change the colour and texture by using contrasting fabrics (see 44) while keeping in touch with the room's overall style. Replace a tired bedhead with panels of material or simply hang a large painting over the bed.

**5 • Fixtures and fittings:** repaint storage units and modernise them with new door furniture for both a visual and tactile makeover.

# 13 blow-the-budget bedrooms

Here are some tempting ideas for delicious extravagance that you might be able to fit into your budget!

## sizing up

Why be content with the existing dimensions of your bedroom? If you can sacrifice an adjoining room, knock through and claim it, either as an en-suite bathroom or as a dressing room/bathroom zone.

## bathing in luxury

Indulge in a spa bath with a separate multi-jet power shower and aromatherapy steam fitting. If space is limited, a Japanese-style square wooden bath is a bespoke alternative (see 17 and 33).

## underfoot

How about a made-to-measure carpet with a smart border (see 68) or a contemporary rug in a design to suit your style (see 69)? And while you are

at it, under-floor heating is not impossibly expensive (see 16 and 66).

## fantasy bed

Get the best quality bed you can and the largest that will happily fit in the room.

## light and sound

A professionally designed lighting system is worth the expense and as rewiring is involved anyway, why not add a state-of-the-art TV and audio system too (see 18 and 91)?

## joinery

Made-to-measure joinery gives you storage that exactly suits your needs and bedroom style (see 85).

## luxurious fabrics

Indulge in luxury fabrics like pure silk, velvet, cashmere, mohair, faux fur, suede and leather (see 44 and 48). There are so many places and ways to use them in a bedroom.

## bespoke creations

Hand-finished curtains are a supreme indulgence, tailored upholstery on a chair or stool looks sophisticated and for a luxurious extra, commission hand-made cushions and bolsters.

# 14

# high-class materials

Introducing top-quality materials will elevate any decorative scheme, even if they're used economically.

## fabric

Cashmere, mohair, faux fur and velvet for throws and cushions and silk for curtains look sumptuous, and suit flannel is great for everything from walls to curtains, chairs to bedcovers.

## bedding

The finest sheets are Egyptian cotton and Irish linen – costly and high-maintenance, but definitely worth it.

## pillows

Lots of plump pillows provides a stylish finish to the well-dressed bed. The softest and most luxurious filling is goose down.

## carpet

All-wool carpets are the best you can buy, or you could indulge in a fun but luxurious-looking deep shag-pile rug (see 68, 69).

## wooden floor

Unusual woods for a floor are brandy-toned Kempsas, pink-tinged Rose Gum Eucalyptus and tea-coloured Merbau.

## leather

The utlimate luxury is leather – tiles and hides for flooring, walls, furniture, panelling and bed-ends, or suede for walls and upholstery.

## wallpaper

Handpainted and bespoke papers are expensive, but just a panel or two will look stunning.

## paint

Suede-effect paint is not expensive but looks luxurious. High-gloss paints that imitate lacquer can be used on plaster, wood and metal.

## glass

Mirrored and glass furniture is making a big comeback. Just one item will add 'edge' to a scheme.

## marble

Marble has always embodied luxury. Choose from highly polished classical marble and 'tumbled' finishes with a tactile, earthy appearance.

# 15

# make a plan

A scale plan is an absolute necessity. It will be your blueprint for all stages, from planning electrical and plumbing works to estimating paint or wallpaper quantities and placing TV and audio systems.

Using graph paper, draw to scale the room's dimensions, doors, windows, radiators, sockets, switches and so on, and make to-scale templates of furniture to see how it will fit in. When your plan is finished, give a copy of it to any contractors.

It's also useful to have a plan of each wall showing doors, windows, skirting boards, alcoves, light switches and wall plugs. This will help you estimate paint, wallpaper and window fabric quantities and shelving and storage requirements. Architectural details such as cornices, panelling and skirting give you a working template for painting.

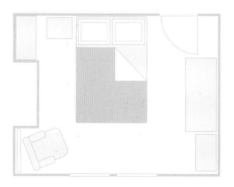

# 16

# heating and ventilation

A comfortable bedroom temperature is 18°c and a bathroom 23°c. An average-sized bedroom needs one radiator but a large room requires more. Ventilation should provide fresh air and control humidity and should be as silent and discreet as possible.

## radiators

Radiators are now an acceptable part of an interior. Modern ones come in all shapes and in finishes from matt black to brilliant chrome. Retro-style radiators suit robust contemporary interiors. If you choose reconditioned radiators make sure they have been properly adapted for modern plumbing.

A radiator is often sited under the window where it works most efficiently but if you have long curtains, you may want to locate it on an interior wall instead. If you inherit a dull radiator, simply camouflage it with paint to match the wall.

## under-floor heating

Most under-floor heating is installed at the building stage, but there are systems that can be laid in isolation, making them an option for a new en suite. There are two types of under-floor heating: a hot-water system runs through flexible piping while an electric one uses wires or matting. Some systems can be integrated with the radiators and certain types can be used with marble, ceramic, stone, vinyl, wood and even carpet.

## ventilation

Air conditioning works well in double-glazed rooms, has flexible temperature control and reduces interior pollution and allergies. Although it doesn't have air-changing qualities, a ceiling fan produces a pleasant breeze.

## humidity

An insulated and air-conditioned environment can be dehydrating. Resolve the problem by having a shallow bowl of water in the room and renewing the water every day. A dehumidifier is a high-tech, noisier option!

## en suite

A bathroom or shower room needs instant heating and ventilation and somewhere to dry towels. A floor- or wall-mounted electric and hot water combination radiator/towel-warmer is a good choice. An extractor fan is vital. Make sure it conforms to regulations.

# 17
# plumbing and electrics

• Have your plan to hand when you consult the electrician and plumber so you can discuss any structural changes and ensure the jobs are carried out in the right order (see 21).
• Having plenty of electric sockets – inside cupboards too – avoids unsightly adaptors and extensions.
• If you are installing double glazing, consider having air conditioning or at least a ceiling fan.
• Make a list of what you need to do and obtain: electric sockets, lights, air conditioning, ceiling fan, ventilation, plumbing for en suite.
• Never attempt to deal with electricity yourself when it comes anywhere near the 'wet' elements of your project!

# 18
# audio and television

A good sound and vision system in the bedroom is a luxury, but once you've got one, you won't look back.

• Make sure you co-ordinate the installation with your other building and decorating works (see 21).
• For comfortable TV viewing a 32cm screen at the end of the bed is adequate, but if the TV is farther away, you will probably want a 52.5cm screen.
• For the best acoustics, have the audio speakers facing something soft – such as the bed.
• We generally watch TV and listen to music at a lower volume in the bedroom, so you won't need big output speakers – will you?
• If you are making an en suite, you might want to install a special audio speaker designed for bathroom use.
• If your system doesn't merit being part of the decorative scheme, build it all into a customised cupboard.
• The simplest audio system for a bedroom is a compact, wall-mounted system.

# 19

## safety matters

More 'home time' hours are spent in the bedroom than in any other room in the house. Minimising the risks from fire, flood, electrical faults and middle-of the-night trips to the bathroom will allow you to sleep in peace.

- Fabrics and bedding materials should be fire retardant and comply with safety standards
- Have fire extinguishers both during and after construction work
- Never leave candles lit at night or if you are out of the room
- Install smoke alarms
- Make sure you have a safety escape and that everyone knows how to use it
- Provide a socket light for night-time use for children and guests
- Never use electrical appliances near water
- Light switches, fixtures and shaving outlets in the bathroom must comply with safety regulations
- Make sure all windows have a locking system and a key that is accessible
- Cupboard doors in children's rooms should have safety catches or childproof catches where necessary
- Regularly check that bunk ladders are stable
- Take care on stepladders when you are accessing high-level storage space
- Use low-odour paints if possible
- Static electricity in synthetic materials such as nylon carpets is considered to be harmful by some people
- Electrical appliances emit radiation and electromagnetic fields unless they are turned off at source

# 20

## finding the right people to help

Creating the bedroom of your dreams is a huge undertaking. Professional help is invaluable, both at the planning/designing stage and for the build itself.

### architect

Use a local certified or chartered architect who will know local contractors. You are not obliged to have the architect find the builder. Architects charge a percentage or an hourly rate but you might be able to negotiate an all-in price. Expect to be invoiced at stages during the work.

### builder

Use a local building firm and go by personal recommendation: what were they like to work with? were they on schedule and within budget? Check on their standard of work via their professional association and to confirm they are financially stable. A smart letter-heading isn't proof. For a big project especially, you might want to check if their professional association has a guarantee scheme against the firm going out of business. Better safe than very cross! Always seek alternative estimates for comparison.

### a bad builder:

- won't be registered for charging and paying VAT
- won't produce properly written quotations
- won't have a registered business address
- won't be able to offer good references
- may not carry proper insurance
- may be unwilling to sign any sort of contract
- is unlikely to employ properly trained labour
- will be unwilling to redress complaints
- will be late, leave early and may not appear at all
- doesn't like to clear up!

## plumber, electrician and joiner

Find either by word of mouth or through your builder. Check references and only employ a fully qualified and registered plumber or electrician.

## interior designer

Find a local one either by recommendation or through their shop, or you may find one from having seen their work in a book, magazine article or advertisement. It's usual to pay travel expenses, a daily rate and a percentage mark-up on sourced materials, furniture and decorative objects.

## soft furnishings maker

Find a soft furnishings maker, curtain maker or upholsterer either by word of mouth, through retail furniture or fabric outlets, or in a large department store with its own making-up service.

# 21

# order of work

Having an understanding of the order in which work should be completed will help your budgeting and time management, as well as providing a template for the contractors so the project can proceed with seamless efficiency!

## structure

- Remove or alter partition walls; erect new ones
- Install new services to 'first fix' (pipes and wires for electricity, telephone, TV, audio, plumbing, central heating, under-floor heating and electric ventilation)
- Strip old wallpaper and repair plaster
- Lay hard flooring
- Repair or install skirting boards and cornices
- Hang new doors and repair or replace window frames and glazing
- Install built-in furniture, bed platform, window seats and so on
- 'Second fix': install and connect radiators, sinks, bath; fix power points and light fittings
- Tiling

## decorating

- Apply undercoat and first coat of paint or line walls and ceiling: this may be done before 'second fix' to prevent naked spots behind radiators
- Final paint finish or hang wallpaper
- Lay carpet
- Install fixed shelving
- Attach curtain poles or rails
- Hang curtains or blinds
- Attach light fittings
- Position bed and furniture
- Add pictures, mirrors and ornaments

part two

# getting down to the detail

# 22 find your look

Creating an inspiration or mood board gives you the opportunity to put together an assortment of decorating materials and stimuli which will help you identify and develop your decorating style.

Take two large sheets of black or dark grey stiff paper or thin board (a dark background 'frames' the materials well). On the first stick, clip or pin intuitive choices taken from your hoard of paint charts, magazines, catalogues and so on. Build on this with ephemeral inspirations, i.e. things you like for their texture or mood but that aren't to be used themselves – a feather, perhaps, or a tortoiseshell button, a scrap of antique material or a leaf skeleton. You could photograph any items that can't be attached to the card. Analysing why you respond positively to each element will help you find the mood of the design. In this way the foundation of your decorative scheme will emerge.

The second board brings the design into focus with real samples and with photographs of hard ingredients, such as radiators, light fittings and storage units. Deal with the main elements first: paint colour, wall and floor coverings, major fabrics and bathroom surfaces, if relevant. Include lots of alternatives so you can mix and match and keep your options open as the scheme comes together. Buy large samples that show the whole pattern repeat and cut them to size according to their proportional use in the bedroom. Observe how colour, pattern and texture relate to each other and to all the other elements such as flooring, furniture and lighting effects. It's a good idea to experiment with paint colours on large pieces of wall-lining paper and hang them in the bedroom to see how the space and light affects them. An important observation is to see how your chosen colours, patterns and textures look in daylight, electric light or candlelight.

# 23 modern comfort

Here quality prevails and no single element dominates. Furniture is comfortable, there is plenty of storage and sumptuous fabrics and textures achieve a dressed-up effect.

## colours

Choose a couple of understated but not monochrome colours and one highlight, such as:
- Caramel, cream and pistachio
- Silver grey, mole, plum
- Ground ginger, chalk and sapphire

## bed

A modern four-poster or large divan gives scope for lavish bed dressing. Top with an oversized bedhead upholstered in a textured fabric.

## walls

In a large room, use pattern – a strongly patterned wallpaper on one wall – or contrasting colour to break up the wall surface. Alternatively, matt and satin paints in the same colour on different walls look subtle.

## window

Generous curtains – perhaps silk mix for the outer curtains and linen for the inner, edged in a contrast fabric – with simple headings.

## flooring

Velvety carpet, such as cut-pile wool (see 67), is a must. For pattern, consider a modern carpet with subtle colour and a quiet design.

## lighting

Thoughtful details – reading lights at just the right height, dimmer switches and accent lights – add the finishing touch.

## furniture

Upholstery should be simple and smart, with the focus on comfort, finish and texture. A chaise longue or easy chair and a dressing table are perfect, while the ideal storage would be a walk-in wardrobe with his and her compartments!

## accessories

Boldness is key – a single beautiful mirror or painting, groups of smaller pictures and one or two oversized ornaments to anchor the whole.

# minimal

A haven of harmony and spaciousness using selective ingredients that are adaptable, comfortable and full of character. If you're able to live with limited furniture and ornamentation, or you're on a tight budget, the minimalist look is for you.

## colours

Go for a very pure monotone scheme, allowing shape and texture to add interest, or use some colour to compensate for minimal furnishing and ornamentation. Strong, but not loud, colour can be used in a controlled way, so harmony is maintained in your palette:

• Chalk white, biscuit, bone, coffee
• Willow-pattern blue, antique silver and chalk
• Moss green, biscuit and lime white

## walls

Use your strong colour with discretion, perhaps on the bed wall only, to emphasise that area. Paint is preferable to wallpaper but you can introduce different paint finishes, such as subtle horizontal stripes of matt and satin. Choose a neutral background shade where you aren't using colour.

## window

You could paint the unadorned window and surround in an accent colour and fit a simple blind or install slatted shutters.

## bed

Sleek and low lines with simple bedclothes that echo the colour theme. Texture is essential, but two contrasts are enough. Alternatively, make the bed the centre of attention: use a lovely antique carved bed perhaps, or a stylish four-poster.

## floor

Bare floorboards are the obvious foundation for the minimalist look. They could be stripped and sealed or given a white colourwash. Rubber tiles, cork or unglazed tiles would be appropriate too.

## lighting

Clever lighting is essential but it doesn't have to be sophisticated. Illuminate the four corners of the room with floor-mounted uplights to maximise the sense of space and use simple, sleek lamps for task and mood lighting. If you have a single special decorative item, spotlight it for impact.

## storage

Maximising storage will eliminate clutter so long as it's easily usable with generous space so that things can be put away without fuss. You could even raise the bed on a box platform with inbuilt storage drawers.

## furniture

One special piece of furniture will set off the look and make a greater contribution than three mundane items! Think of shape and colour, no matter whether the piece is modern or a battered antique.

## accessories

Pictures look great in uniform frames hung in a geometric block. Add a large mirror with a broad frame to accentuate the feeling of spaciousness and spotlight a single, spectacular flower in a brightly coloured vase.

# 25 zen zone

Western comfort and convenience infuse the serenity of a traditional Japanese sleeping zone. There is emphasis on surfaces, natural materials feature above colour, and refined shape and line create harmony and space.

## colours

Indigo blue is traditionally the key colour, with other colour coming from natural materials and black and white highlights. Choose additional colours, like jade green, to promote serenity.
• Indigo blue, porcelain white, bamboo
• Rice white, ebony, maple
• Jade green, ivory, grey, black lacquer

## window

Simple white blinds are best or, for texture, grass fibre, pinoleum or bamboo. Translucent paper screens provide privacy but filter the light.

## bed

Replace the traditional futon on tatami mats with a plain blond-wood bed on low legs or 'floating' on a base, or by a sleeping platform enclosed by sliding screens. Dress the bed with bolsters and plain bed coverings.

## walls

Emphasising space and light are essential to the Zen look, so white painted walls are perfect, with perhaps a natural grass paper for texture and interest on one wall.

## floor

Dark-stained floorboards are ideal but tiles also work. Mats are the traditional floor covering, but seagrass, jute or sisal carpets are all suitable alternatives.

## lighting

White or off-white lamp shades in paper, opaque parchment or ceramic suit the theme.

## storage

Cupboards with frosted glass, polypropylene or paper-faced sliding doors imitate rice-paper screens, or you might install shelves and hanging rails covered with plain white blinds.

## furniture

Japanese furniture is low to the ground. All you need in the bedroom is a single wooden bench and a couple of X-frame bedside stools.

## accessories

Meditation on nature is at the heart of Zen – a branch of cherry blossom in a slim vase, a mound of polished pebbles in a simple dish, a beautiful Japanese landscape painting or a calligraphy scroll on the wall.

# 26 girly heaven

Bright and casual, this feminine bedroom is full of pattern, texture and fun! Colours and styles are mixed together to create a sumptuous and sexy boudoir. Whimsy and intuition are all you need to get it right.

## colours

Weave a thread of continuity through the mix of colours by using a little more of one colour in your palette of choice such as lilacs and pinks or citrus and orange.

## bed

Naturally, the bed is the focus, piled high with layers of pretty floral covers, quilts and lacy pillows. Add a soft throw and a tasselled satin bolster or two. For added princess effect, surround the bed with coloured and crystal-trimmed sheer drapes or panels hung from dainty poles attached to the ceiling with hooks and ribbons.

## window

Cover the window with a sheer, bright panel to tint the filtered daylight. Add an outer, over-long curtain in a sumptuous fabric and create a simple window seat padded with cushions.

## walls

Paint provides the flexibility you need when you fancy changing one colour to match another within the scheme. It's a good idea not to paint all the walls in one strong colour, as this will make a room feel smaller.

## lighting

The lighting should be feminine and eccentric: a pretty chandelier, wall brackets with crystal drops, strings of fairy or rope lights circumnavigating the room and scented candles in lanterns and coloured glass holders.

## floor

As you will spend lots of time in bare feet trying on clothes in the bedroom, it's vital to have a warm floor. Go overboard with a shag-pile carpet and your feet will thank you. Alternatively, invest in large, strategically placed flokati rugs.

## storage

Show off your best party frocks by displaying them on padded hangers on a coat stand or screen. If there is a shortage of regular cupboard space, use large boxes covered in a pretty paper or fabric instead.

## furniture

A dressing table with plenty of drawer space for cosmetics is important of course, plus a pretty mirror, light and an upholstered stool to sit on. Add to these a capacious bedside cupboard, a full-length swivel mirror and a deeply comfortable 'gossiping' chair.

## accessories

Mount photographs together within large frames and create a gallery space on one wall; group items of memorabilia together for display impact; store and show off pretty shoes on low open shelves.

# 27
## urban loft

Imaginative zoning creates multi-functional open-plan sleeping with an integrated bath or shower room. Surprisingly, the style can be adapted to modest spaces.

### space
In a large space use low-level dividers – half-walls, large pieces of multi-functional furniture – to maintain a visual flow, or go for a change in floor level. In a more limited space, choose sliding screens or fabric hangings.

### materials
Accentuate the 'loft' theme with judicious use of wood, brick and glass – brick cladding on one wall with the others simply plastered and painted, glass bricks to screen a bathing area.

### lighting
Keep windows clutter free and use overhead 'bare wire' tracks that allow lights to be moved to different areas. Wall uplights will illuminate the textural qualities of the architecture.

### floor
A loft is the place to be adventurous with flooring. Choose from wood, concrete, ceramic, linoleum, vinyl and rubber, each with its pluses and minuses. Wood, for example needs regular polishing and waxing. Concrete has the right look but is noisy and heavy, so is suitable for ground-floor and basement areas only. Ceramic comes in a huge range of prices and styles, but is also noisy and heavy. Rubber is great for the loft look and maintenance is easy, but light colours show the dirt.

# 28
## city slicker

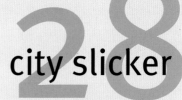

Handsome, sophisticated and immaculately dressed are the words that describe this look. Pared-down and deeply comfortable, this bedroom is functional and tailored, without frivolous ornamentation. It features strong materials such as wood, leather and metal, combined with plain but tactile fabrics.

### colour
Dark, warm colours give an aura of comfortable sophistication. However, dark colours need to be offset with areas of light: here white bed linen is the natural contrast. In addition, deeper colours are also lifted with touches of metallic glitz. Colour combinations to set the mood:
• Charcoal, silver and moss green
• Mushroom, midnight blue and cream
• Plum, old gold, black and ivory

### materials
With the emphasis on masculinity, fabrics such as jumbo corduroy, heavy linen and suit flannel would make a good team for the bed dressing. Battening some fabric to the walls will create a den-like cosiness: consider

strong, tactile materials such as faux suede or felt, defining the tailoring with a narrow gimp or ribbon along the ceiling and skirting board.

## window

The tailored look could be continued with clean-cut curtains in felt or corduroy hanging from chunky poles threaded through huge eyelet holes. Alternatively, wooden slatted blinds or shutters would be equally suitable.

## floor

If there is a wooden floor, you might add a touch of cowboy with a couple of cow-skin rugs. Leather is a luxury flooring option, and could be used as a fixed 'raft' just around the bed. For a softer effect, opt for a wool carpet that imitates jute or sisal.

## lighting

For this bachelor environment, wall-mounted lights on swivel arms might be more practical and appropriate than regular bedside lamps. Likewise, downlights and interior cupboard lighting do away with unnecessary

freestanding lights. Don't forget the dimmer switches!

## storage

The joy of living the bachelor life is that your storage can be designed to suit your suits! Make sure you have shelving that is capacious rather than over-segmented and don't forget to include a full-length mirror in your cupboard planning.

## washing

With many fabrics in the room, steam from an integrated washing area might present problems. The ideal set-up is to separate washing from clothes storage with an enclosed passageway containing built-in cupboards and shelves. In a limited space, installing a large and powerful shower unit may be a better option than a bath.

# 29 floral update

The new floral bedroom uses light flower-patterned fabrics and plains with subtle contrasting checks and stripes. Anchor it all with timeless detailing – lined and trimmed curtains, tailored cushions and smartly upholstered furniture.

## colours

Choose well-proportioned combinations of floral colours so that one won't dominate the scheme or go for a single-colour scheme based on a toile de Jouy or a monochromatic flower design combined with a coloured stripe and another small geometric pattern. Possible floral colour combinations include:
• Peppermint, raspberry and cream
• Primrose, iris blue and snowdrop white
• Shades of lilac and aqua

## materials

Glazed chintz is the classic floral fabric but there are many modern updates such as unglazed cotton, linen mixes and silk. The key is lightweight fabric and the use of reflective surfaces here and there to bring out the colours' vibrancy.

## pattern

Single-flower motifs look their best as curtaining. If the pattern is strong, don't use it again especially if the room is on the small side, but instead choose a counter-pattern on a smaller scale for the bedcover. Cushions are a useful method of re-introducing the main floral fabrics on a small scale or choose a cushion with a photographic botanical print. Use areas of plain-coloured and neutral materials to link the florals.

## floor

Flooring needs to be a strong counterpoint to the pattern and fabric. It could be as dramatic as unglazed tiles in a pale limestone colour, or simply blonde wood. If you have old floorboards, you might take pity on them and strip, fill, colourwash and varnish them. Add one of the many contemporary rugs in subtle toning colours to provide a soft touch for the feet!

# retro 30

One retro-style bedroom design approach mixes flavours from various periods, rather than creating a focused period scheme. This highly personalised bedroom look should evolve after the decorative foundations are in place, as it needs objects and furnishings that must be sourced from many places. The look infuses references from the twenties through to the seventies, depending on preference and budget, to produce an eclectic balance. The second approach is to concentrate on a more specific period, such as the fifties, and create a bedroom scheme that supports this style using the colour, pattern and texture that are appropriate to the period.

## colour

The best way to introduce colour to a retro bedroom is through the use of decorative objects and furnishings. Anything goes because variety is part of the scheme, so choose colours according to your favourite era, from pink to scarlet, acid green to luminous turquoise, or orange and brown – heaven help you! However, the more colour you introduce, the less you'll need on the walls and in the flooring. To prevent the bedroom becoming claustrophobic, keep walls and flooring mainly neutral and low key.

## walls

If you are focusing on objects from different periods, a warm, neutral colour for the walls makes a safe background. Alternatively, use a subtle geometric wallpaper – softly abstract circles or rounded rectangles. Hessian wallpaper adds texture and warmth and is reminiscent of seventies style.

## floor

Flooring materials are really a matter of budget and style. Black- or white-painted and varnished floorboards or plain white tiles, vinyl, parquet, square felt carpet tiles or shag pile carpet all provide their own period reference. Otherwise, invest in a large rug whose colour and design conveys the period you have chosen.

## furniture and accessories

Eclectic inspiration from the twenties to the seventies might include mirrored bedside tables, a metalwork dressing table, an Arne Jacobsen-style moulded plywood-and-steel chair, a multi-branched floor light, a melamine chest of drawers with round tapered legs, a teak and twine ceiling light, a sunburst mirror and Savoy or 'handkerchief' vases. For the bed itself, depending on period, choose a mirror-panelled headboard or a rectangular or elliptic deep-padded bedhead.

# 31 two into one will go dual-purpose bedrooms

Sometimes you have no choice but to incorporate different functions into a bedroom. The most extreme example is a studio bedroom or bedsit. Then there's the bedroom with washing facilities, the bedroom that doubles as a study, and finally, the bedroom/guest room. Whichever you require, don't despair: where there is a will, there is a way of making it fit!

## zone or harmonise?

If you have a lot of space, you can zone the room with half-height or full-height partitions. To minimise light loss go for toughened, translucent glass panels, glass bricks or a fabulous screen. Other ideas include using a freestanding shelf unit or enclosing the bed with a half-height wall that doubles as a headboard. Alternatively, use different flooring for different activities – rubber flooring next to the kitchen cabinets and hardwood and a rug for the living area.

If space is at a premium, harmonise the room rather than zone it: use the same wood for cupboards in the kitchen and the rest of the room, the same flooring material throughout, the same colour theme for kitchen accessories, throws and cushions. If you keep things simple you won't notice just how much is crammed into one small space.

## conceal

In a multi-function room, some concealment is essential, which is where purpose-built joinery comes into its own. A small kitchen or study area can be closed off behind floor-to-ceiling sliding or folding doors. Or stow your computer and keyboard on a pull-out shelf inside a cupboard. Have the cupboard specially made or adapt a chain-store cupboard to suit. Add some clip-on task lighting, and you're ready for action, but remember to plan the power points before the cupboard is irrevocably fixed!

## use the height

Don't forget the areas above eye-level. If your room has plenty of height, put your bed on a platform with cupboards – and perhaps a sofa – beneath. And if you've got space, you could build a room within a room. The bed is on top with steps – providing extra storage – leading from the kitchen or bathroom (or both) downstairs. The surrounding space plays host to your dining and relaxing.

## fold, stack and stow

So many new homes consist of small rooms that furniture designers have come up with some lovely space-saving ideas. For starters, there are good-looking fold-away and stacking tables – like your grandmother's. Then there are beds with storage beneath (see 78 and 89) as well as a whole host of stacking and folding chairs – remember the school hall?

# 32

# the studio

This is the room that has it all. It's where you sleep, cook, relax, eat and do your homework. There's no escaping it: you have to be tidy.

## the bed

You may have screened off your bed or put it up on a platform (see 31), but if these options don't suit, there are others that may. First there's the futon bed that doubles as a sofa, or the more traditional sofa bed with a foam or inner-sprung mattress on a wood and metal frame that simply slides and swivels into place (see 78). Finally, there's the all-singing, all-dancing pull-down bed in a cabinet that usually includes storage and sometimes a fold-down workspace too.

## fabrics

With lots of hard materials in the kitchen area, make the most of fabrics elsewhere. Velvet, cord and faux suede look sensational on the sofa or bed, and cashmere throws or a suede footstool-cum-coffee table make great finishing touches.

## colour

In a large bedroom, colour can delineate an area: a tranquil, neutral bed zone graduating to stronger tones in the kitchen. But if the room is small, keep the colour theme unified throughout (see 31).

## lighting

You need a mixture of background, task and accent lighting, but avoid harsh solitary overhead lights. Use downlights for general and accent lighting, wall-washing uplights to expand the space and task lights for working in the kitchen and for reading and office work.

## pattern

You need to be careful how you use pattern or every time you go in your studio, you'll wish you hadn't. Avoid wallpaper or fabric with a dominating pattern – it will have to fight with everything else – and instead go for restrained, symmetrical designs that will help create a decorative rhythm and be easy on the eye. Or simply stick to plain colour and bring in little doses of pattern here and there.

# 33 bed and bath

It wasn't so very long ago that houses had no indoor bathroom, but nowadays it seems, the more you've got, the more you want. The ideal second (or third) bathroom is an en suite but if you don't have the space you may find room for a shower in the bedroom or at least a washbasin.

## where and how?

In a large bedroom, you can make an en suite by adding a partition wall and a door or, if you don't mind less privacy, you could simply have an archway. Alternatively you might choose to break through into an adjoining room, but check with an architect or surveyor first to make sure that it's safe to do so.

## tiny spaces

A shower cubicle can be fitted into the smallest bedroom. If you are having made-to-measure cupboards, you might consider plumbing in a shower behind a cupboard front for that now-you-see-it now-you-don't effect. But if a shower is really not feasible, at least fit a tiny washbasin, just for the convenience of shaving, face washing and teeth brushing.

## the wet room

For the ultimate in contemporary design, you have to have a wet room – a radical option and not to all tastes. It can either be screened from the bedroom or integrated in it. All you need is a fabulous modern power shower with a securely sealed tiled floor with drainage channels. If the idea appeals to you, you must consult an architect because there are lots of structural issues involving weight and waterproofing. If you can't bear to be parted from your bath, opt for a freestanding bath in the bedroom instead – roll-top for a traditional look, or glass, wood or steel if you're into minimalism.

## the boring details

Boring they may be, but no one can afford to ignore issues of plumbing, heating, electricity and ventilation. First, water must be brought to the en suite and waste carried away. Then you must ensure that your central heating can cope with any extra radiators (or install under-floor heating) and of course you need electricity for lighting, shaving sockets and perhaps an electrically heated towel rail. And as water and electricity don't mix, you'll definitely need to use a professional installer. And last but not least, think about ventilation issues – especially if your en suite doesn't have a window. You don't want unpleasant smells wafting into the bedroom, or the make-up mirror steaming up all the time.

## storage

En suites have their special storage problems but as they say, necessity is the mother of invention. You need to think about where to keep spare towels, toilet rolls and toiletries, as well as cleaning materials and reading matter for those private moments on the toilet. Think under-basin storage, clever shelving, above-the-door 'dead' areas as well as a range of decorative bowls, baskets and boxes for a personal touch.

# mixing work with pleasure

Your bedroom may be where you do a bit of paperwork or it might be where you earn your living. Don't worry if you can't hide your equipment away or if you can't have a dedicated work area (see 31), there are other possibilities.

## desk

Choose a beautiful table that doesn't necessarily say 'desk'. Think antique side tables, old kitchen tables, glass dining tables, even a small cloth-covered trestle table.

## computer

Not all computers are boring beige bricks. Watch out for sleek metal finishes, black and juicy-fruit colours, and flat screens. There's something new every six months so there's bound to be one that you will be proud to have on show. And if not, then read on.

## screen it off

Put work out of sight and out of mind with a panel that fixes to the wall or a flexible wooden screen that snakes around awkward shapes and takes up less room than a rigid screen.

## filling corners

Create a mini-workstation in a wasted corner. Fit a triangular shelf with a cupboard beneath as a desk, and more triangular shelves above for storage.

## filing facts

Have plenty of attractive shelving and use it to store paperwork in matching file boxes, or disguise the shelves with doors or roller blinds.

## health matters

Working can seriously damage your health and there are special issues to consider if you work in your bedroom. Arrange your workstation to benefit from natural light, have good task lighting and angle the computer screen away from the window. An ergonomic work stool is more comfortable than an ordinary chair and takes up less room. And last but not least, keep electronic equipment to a minimum because electrical appliances emit radiation and electromagnetic fields. If possible, cables shouldn't live under the bed and everything ought to be turned off at source when not in use.

# guests-to-go 35

When it comes to accommodating a guest, you may be lucky enough to have a dedicated guest bedroom, but sometimes housing a guest can mean some ingenious thinking.

## the bed

In a dedicated guest room, a 137cm double bed is adequate for a short-stay couple. A more flexible alternative is a pair of zip-linked single beds, stacking beds or a single bed with a pull-out extension. In a multi-purpose room, a sofa bed, futon (see 78), or pull-down bed (see 78) may be better.

## washing

If there are no en-suite bathing facilities, a small basin in the room lots of fluffy towels, a screen around the basin and a towelling bathrobe will be very welcome.

## privacy

Make sure there is adequate screening at the windows and don't forget to have a lock on the inside of the door, especially if there are washing facilities in the room.

## storage

Your guest will need to hang and fold a few clothes. Provide a small cupboard or, failing that, a hat stand, hooks or a wooden towel rail.

## comforts

Provide a good reading light and a task light next to a mirror. A bedside table with an alarm clock, magazines, flowers, tissues and a decanter is a specially nice touch.

## what a squeeze!

You'd be surprised where a guest can be accommodated. Do you have a half-landing big enough to become a sleeping niche? If you do, install a mattress or foam cushions on a slatted wooden base and when not in use as a bed, it can be a window seat. To make the space more private, have curtains that can enclose it.

Or have you got 'dead' space under-the-stairs? If it's large enough, build a cabin bed, with under-bed cupboards and shelves above. Cosy lighting completes the scene.

# 36

## the language of colour

Our perception of and reaction to colour is a subjective business: one person's 'exquisitely subtle lilac' will be another's 'wishy-washy purple'. But the reality is that different colours and the way they are used create certain moods, change a room's perspective and subconsciously conjure up particular associations that have the most profound influence on interior style. In the bedroom context, colour is pivotal in creating the right atmosphere, from cosy to cosmopolitan, soothing to sexy. Knowing how colour works will help you find just the right colour to suit your mood.

### 10 ideas

### knowing your tints from your tones

• Complementary colours are diametrically opposite: red to green, yellow to violet and blue to orange; obviously, there are lots of graduated colours between these.
• Intensity or saturation refers to colour strength. A pure colour (hue) has the highest intensity; adding grey or a complementary colour will reduce intensity.
• Tint is produced by adding white to the pure colour, reducing its strength: pink is a tint of red.
• Shade is produced by adding black to pure colour, reducing its vividness: maroon is a shade of red.
• Tone refers to graduation from cool to warm and to lightness or darkness: pale pink to wine red, for example.

### principle practice

Base, tone and accent are the three principles of colour use: the base is the most used colour, the secondary colour is a tone of the base and the third is an unrelated colour. Two example schemes could be lavender, purple and silver-grey, or putty, coffee and brick red.

### three-colour trick

If you're anxious about choosing a range of colours, it's safe to stick to a three-colour palette to start with and then add other colours over time as your confidence increases.

### nice neutrals

Calming neutral colours come in a great range of greys, browns, beiges, whites, and would make a sophisticated bedroom choice. However, neutrals need material texture and accent colour to animate the scheme.

### keeping things simple

Monochromatic schemes are composed of one colour in different guises – either in lighter or darker tones. These help the visual flow and will create a harmonious, soothing bedroom. A palette of different colours with equal tones will be harmonious and easy to use so long as you get the subtle balance of colours right.

### soothing tones

Cool colours such as violet-blues, green-blues and blue-greens optically 'recede', promoting a sense of space and serenity. Surprisingly, there are also cool pinks and yellows but you need to have good natural and artificial light to prevent these from becoming cold.

## pretty in pastel

Pastels provide a calming palette for the bedroom but used together over a large area they can look insipid. To avoid this, anchor the scheme with stronger colour accents such as darker skirting boards and window frames. As the scheme develops, you can introduce other colour accents within the soft furnishings and ornamentation.

## deeply handsome

Dark colours such as charcoal, moss green, midnight blue, aubergine, cinnamon and chocolate all help to create an intimate and sensual environment. If your bedroom is naturally dark and you're not looking for the illusion of space, those colours are smart bedroom choices, but set them off with some light, bright or white contrasts.

## primary colours

Intense colours such as primary yellow and red are tricky to use in the bedroom as they optically 'advance' and tend to make a small room claustrophobic. To avoid this you could use one colour on a single wall. This would usually be behind the bed to lend focus there, but there is no reason why a different wall couldn't be painted, especially if you wanted to make a strong backdrop for paintings or ornaments.

## what you see is not necessarily what you get!

Always experiment with a lighter tone or two than your first choice colour because paint colour will usually look darker over a large area of wall. All colour is visually changed by natural light, electric lighting, texture and surface finish, so it's a good idea to try out colours in the room before committing yourself.

# neutral schemes 37

Although the true neutral colours are black, white and grey, the range used in decorating is more extensive. Best for the bedroom are warm-tinted neutrals, which include chalk, cream, bone, pearl, ivory, limestone, biscuit, parchment, sand, toffee, camel and mushroom.

A neutral-coloured bedroom is easy on the eye and promotes tranquillity and relaxation. Try using different, but tonally balanced, neutrals together in varying proportions or subtle grey and white combinations.

Introducing a minor colour accent or two prevents blandness: cushions and a bed throw are obviously versatile choices. Experimenting with any single favourite colour will reveal the different effects. Charcoal or black could be the defining contrast for grey and white schemes perhaps for a headboard border, lampshades or lacquered bedside tables. Pure white cotton or linen is a perfect finish for bedding. Provide visual focus with a stunning painting, flowers or an ornate mirror.

Texture and neutrals complement each other beautifully and attention paid to underscoring these contrasts will benefit the scheme. Try placing rough and smooth, shiny and matt, heavy and fine in juxtaposition. In addition or as an alternative to the textural focus, appropriate patterns might include muted flowing designs such as a monochromatic crewelwork, damask, scrolling and self-patterned fabrics and wallpapers.

With so many neutral-coloured possibilities it's easy to harmonise a neutral bedroom scheme with the en suite. Bathroom neutrals include limestone, terrazzo, marble, biscuit-glazed tiles and painted or limed tongue-and-groove panelling. Using a neutral colour focus throughout helps to soften and blend hard edges and surfaces.

The bedroom is a perfect environment for mixing neutral colours, pattern and texture as there are so many elements to associate them with without upsetting the decorative rhythm: mix them with earthy materials such as stone, wicker, bamboo and rattan; fabrics like linen, silk and mohair and organic flooring such as sisal, jute and seagrass. ·

# 38
# fresh schemes

The fresh bedroom scheme is based on crisp, clean light colours that are carefree, restorative and easy on the eye.

Combined with lots of white, shades of blue and green work well together when they are of the same tonal range. Try painting the walls in blocks of chalky blue, aqua and lilac for a soft patchwork effect or use the colours on walls, ceiling, painted furniture and architectural detailing.

Blue and white are always a popular combination as are the sunshine colours yellow and blue, but choose these with care – a primrose yellow with a red-touched blue – or the yellow can look quite cold. You might introduce some elements of grey as a tempering influence.

Metallic and shiny finishes are good companions for the fresh colour palette. Silver paint can be 'tinted' with an undercoat of lilac or blue, revealed when the silver is 'rubbed off' slightly.

Fabrics must be light to maintain the freshness of the look. Go for plain lightweight taffeta, silk mixes and sheers for window panels and dressing the bed. And pattern must be unfussy – a crisp, simple flower print, a two-toned geometric, an unfussy floral motif together with plains, checks and stripes for upholstery and cushions.

Artificial lighting needs the brightness of halogen downlights combined with soft wall-washing from low-level uplights.

A sense of space and light is best maintained by having simple window treatments – unlined fabric panels with tab tops in a sheer or patterned print are a good choice – and minimal ornamentation. However, mirrored furniture or oversized mirrors on the wall will reflect and accentuate the room's light and colour.

# 39

# bright schemes

We associate bright colours with exotic travel to India, Morocco, Mexico and the Caribbean. The colour range includes the three primaries – red, blue and yellow – and a host of shades in between, from hot pink to orange, lettuce green to turquoise, banana yellow to imperial purple.

You could choose a single colour such as cornflower blue or lacquer red as the principal player, perhaps painted on one wall and outlined with a darker colour. Paint or paper the other walls in a neutral shade – silver grey as a counterpoint to the red, biscuit to the blue. For a softer, subtler look, create your own colours in tinted acrylic or oil glaze, which gives you control over the intensity of colour and a depth to the finish that is lacking in standard emulsion paint.

A brightly coloured palette is fun but you must take care in small

spaces and where the light is cold as bright colours will decrease the sense of space. You will also need plenty of versatile electric lighting, as bright colours can look heavy in low, flat light.

Bright colours can also be used against a relatively neutral background. Introduce them in your bed linen, cushions, throws, lamps and decorative objects.

Another way to use bright colour is on window frames, skirting boards and doors or, for a fun contemporary look, choose an unusual floor covering such as rubber tiles, in a vivid colour.

Hot, bright colour generates vitality and creativity, so it's good for a working area in a bedroom. If nothing else, you might choose a brightly coloured desk chair and filing accessories.

And finally, as a foil, always include ample areas of neutral colour: the floor is the obvious place – think wood, glazed tiles or woven sisal for a strong but cool visual base.

# dark schemes

Dark, moody colours give a bedroom a sophisticated, smartly dressed look. This colour range includes charcoal, ash grey, moleskin, cinnamon, chocolate, midnight blue, moss green, plum, damson and aubergine. Choose dark colours to cocoon a small bedroom that is lacking in natural light, or use them as a dramatic backdrop for imaginative bed dressing and glamorous furniture and ornaments.

Dark colours complement other dark colours to spectacular effect, but benefit from lighter, brighter touches to maximise their impact and vigour and prevent any hint of oppressiveness. Introduce white or neutral elements and touches of 'sparkle' in the form of contrast colour, metallic detailing and creative lighting. Effective schemes to consider include:
• Prussian blue walls; charcoal, midnight blue and white bedding

with metallic grey cushions; charcoal paintwork with antique silver highlights in furniture and architectural details. Greyhound grey-and-blue bordered felt curtains hung from antiqued silver-painted poles. Pigeon-grey carpet.
• Damson glaze-finished walls or a wine-red damask wallpaper; flat black woodwork; wood louvred blinds or shutters; old gold highlights in ornamental detail; ivory bedding with chocolate covers; floorboards in similar wood finish as blinds or shutters.
• Ivy green mid-sheen painted walls or a wallpaper with a flowing two-tone green pattern; mushroom and coffee with cream bed dressing; mushroom velvet cord curtains; bronze finishing details and accessories; natural flooring such as jute or sisal.

If you use dark colour in a vertical block, for instance on a single wall, you could reintroduce it in a horizontal form, as an area rug or a bedspread for example, and add another touch or two elsewhere, such as a couple of cushions and a lampshade. These small details are

perfect for helping to settle the eye and create visual rhythm.

The effect of lighting on dark colour can be spectacular. Use floor-mounted uplights in corners to ensure that the dark colour doesn't end up black. Small downlights provide sparkle, while spotlights focus on decorative objects or paintings (see 56). Bedside lighting might be wall-mounted bracket lamps or bedside table lights (see 55). And don't forget the magic of candlelight gleaming on lustrous dark walls and catching the metallic highlights.

# 41
# muted schemes

Muted colours are generally created with a touch of black or grey added to the base colour. For bedroom use, the most suitable colours include dusty rose, plaster pink, sage green, French grey and Swedish blue: these colours are naturally affiliated with French chateaux and Swedish homesteads. There are other kindred colours, including earthy mustard, terracotta and Shaker blue green, but they are rather heavy for bedroom decoration.

French grey is somewhere between grey, blue and green, which makes an easy-on-the-eye background colour for walls. Dusty rose partners this colour beautifully as curtains and bed covers. To emphasise the French theme, you might use a toile de Jouy, whose pictorial print represents 18th-century pastoral scenes. Alternatively, select embroidery weaves or small florals that have plenty of white in them.

A sleigh bed or lit bateau would be ideal, hung with checked or flower-sprig silk drapes from a ceiling 'corona' (see 82). To complete the chateau look include white painted furniture with gilt detailing, large rococo-style mirrors, candlelight wall brackets and a crystal chandelier. Alternatively, create a fusion look with thoroughly modern furniture in pale wood and glass. The floor could be white painted or sanded with an Aubusson-style needlepoint rug in dusty rose and sage green tones.

Alternatively, the muted scheme could be developed using Swedish blue as its foundation colour. Paint the walls matt bone white and create 'frames' of grey blue in varying widths of stripe-within-stripe as a fantasy panelling effect. The curtain fabric could be a combined stripe and flower motif to fall in loose lengths onto the floor. A bed with a decorative wooden high head and footboard would suit the look dressed with a puffy duvet and quilt with a blue-and-white check. Furniture could follow the theme but extend the colouring in blond wood or white and sage green paint. Limed and waxed timber flooring could be softened with white cotton runners or a natural weave rug contrast-bound around the edges.

# 42 talk about texture

Texture is as significant as colour and pattern to good interior design. Textures can be combined in many ways and in fact, bedrooms and en suites are the best rooms for maximising the use of texture as there is so much variety of materials to play with (see 43).

## looking for texture

You may be surprised to learn that texture is everywhere. It is found not only in fabrics but in paint finishes, wallpaper, carpet, leather, metal, wood, brick, stone and glass, so indulge!

## the elements of texture

Texture can be rough, smooth, opaque, sheer, matt or glossy and can also be divided into 'cool' and 'warm'. Cool textures include smooth, light-reflective surfaces such as satin, silk, gloss paint, glazed tiles and glass; warm ones include matt, light-absorbing surfaces – linen, mohair, faux suede, limestone and natural wood are good examples.

## keep hold

Some colours – neutrals for instance – 'hold' texture better than others.

## textural pattern

Texture creates its own pattern and can introduce a sense of geometry and balance.

## sensuality

Exploit a material's texture – put velvet, silk or lambswool on the bed so you can touch it or have an open-weave linen panel at the window so light filtering through creates a pattern on the floor.

## en-suite texture

Hard textures such as tile, metal and porcelain inevitably dominate in a bathroom and en suite so include some softening ones for contrast – rush matting and bath mats, towels and sheer curtains.

## restrictions apply

In the bedroom, restrict the use of hard materials such as stone, brick and tiles to maintain a sense of peace and harmony.

## light

Textures look different according to the light. Flat lighting diminishes their subtlety. Uplights and side-lighting are most effective.

## textural links

For a textural link between the bedroom and en suite, make use of textural echoes. Have the same wood for bedroom furniture and bathroom cabinets, or matt and glossy paint in the same colour and proportions. Or differentiate the two zones with hard, glossy surfaces for the en suite and soft and matt materials in the bedroom.

## dampening off

The dampness of the bathroom means many textural fabrics and soft flooring materials are out of bounds, but enjoy those which don't mind getting damp around the edges, such as luxurious towelling and rush flooring.

**10 ideas**

# texture in the bedroom and the en suite

## fabric choices

The bed naturally provides the main stage on which to use textured fabrics, but lots of different ones together can just be too much. Choose one or two as highlights and only use for cushions or upholstery.

## wall street

Wall coverings offer another huge range of textural possibilities. Depending on the look you want in the bedroom, choose from grass fibre, hessian, metallic and matt-textured wallpapers, contrasting matt and sheen paint or suede-effect paint, and polished plaster. En-suite choices include tile, stone or metal cladding and wood. Combinations of clear and etched glass and mirror are also effective

## floor mania

In the bedroom the choices include wood, tiles, leather and rubber, all of which can be softened with rugs or mats. Natural floorings include sisal, jute, seagrass, thick tatami or thin Goza mats (see 69). In the en suite exploit hard flooring – terrazzo and mosaic for texture with pattern, slate with its subtle ridges. Textured rubber is practical as well as visually interesting. And don't forget the fluffy bath mat!

# textural combinations for that 'wow!' factor

Finding the right partnerships among textured ingredients should be as much fun as mixing colour and pattern. The joy of using texture in the bedroom – not forgetting that textures are found in wall finishes, flooring and hard components as well as fabrics – is in finding just the right combinations for a tactile and sensuous mélange that underlines your individual bedroom style. So don't feel restrained in your choices, but seek out interesting, even eccentric, ingredients to give your scheme a designer's edge.

## updated deco

For a contemporary echo of twenties art deco, which plays on matt and shiny surfaces.
• Painted matt-and-lustre horizontally striped walls
• Modern abstract appliqué curtains
• Satin quilt
• Mirrored furniture
• Stripped matt-varnished floorboards
• Self-patterned mixed-pile rug

## urban loft

Tactile but strong textural combinations wrapped up in a shell of gleaming plaster:
• Polished plaster walls
• Jumbo cord curtains
• Wool and suede on the bed
• Contrast-coloured jumbo cord and tweed cushions with bone buttons
• Luxurious loop-pile carpet

## morocco bound

Keep a richly textural but neutral background and make the bed the focus of brightly coloured mixed-media textures:
• Parchment-effect wallpaper
• Sheer, bright fabric hanging behind the bed
• Patterned-silk bedspread
• Mirrored and bauble-trimmed fabric for cushions and satin-tasselled bolsters
• Fretwork window screens
• Jute carpet on patterned tiled floor

## new damask and silk

Damask's all-over pattern makes a handsome textural partner for sensational 'creased' fabrics at the window:
• Modern damask wallpaper
• 'Creased' silk fabric curtains
• Matt faux suede-covered bed
• Satin sheets, wool blankets

## matt and shiny

A neutral scheme allows textural contrasts to play against each other for maximum effect:
• Grass-fibre wallpaper
• Wooden slatted window blinds
• Neutral-coloured satin bedhead
• Matelassé quilt
• Animal-skin print carpet

# 45

## play with pattern

Pattern is complex. We react intuitively to it, so make your response your starting point. If you like a dominant pattern, use it to dictate the room's style, or choose a pattern that is easily integrated in a variety of schemes.

### bedroom choices

Bedroom fabrics offer plenty of pattern opportunities. Obvious favourites are florals, checks and stripes, but pattern is also in textural fabrics such as chenille, quilting and matelassé. Finally, there are fabrics such as lace and printed or appliqué sheers which need light to reveal their pattern.

### pattern partners

Proportion and harmony are key for successful pattern marriages. Stripes, checks and florals are natural partners, while spot, lozenge and small motifs

socialise with almost any larger pattern. Toile de Jouy, crewelwork and Chinoiserie usually take centre stage.

### showing style

Pattern helps to signpost a particular decorative style: a muted floral fabric leads it in one direction, a sassy geometric wallpaper in another.

### in a mood

Pattern helps create a certain mood, whether sensual, playful, dramatic, feminine, masculine, cosy or sophisticated. Emphasise the effect by your choice of colour and texture – dark, matt and heavy for masculine; pastel, shiny and translucent for feminine.

### colour coding

Pattern is easier to use when the colour range is restricted. For a restrained, harmonious scheme use neutral-coloured, subtle patterns such as stamped and appliquéd fabrics, damask and monochrome crewelwork.

### creating rhythm

Bedroom patterns should be easy on the eye, so go for symmetrical or repetitive designs and broad horizontal lines rather than busy pattern.

### proportional representation

Depending on their size, stripes can elongate or diminish length and width, while a bold design will break up a large expanse of wall.

### pattern as a disguise

Rhythmically patterned wallpaper such as toile de Jouy or a flowing floral design will disguise a room's awkward angles.

### finding focus

Pattern can lead the eye around the room and draw it to a focal point. It can also appear discreetly in lampshades, cushions, upholstery or a decorative vase or rug.

### tile claustrophobia

Avoid an excess of patterned tiles in an en suite or the effect will be claustrophobic. Bear in mind that the smaller the tiles, the more 'pattern' there will be.

## 10 rules

# 46 put pattern in its place

## how much can you take?

If you have a large bedroom, combine a dominant wallpaper pattern with smaller patterns for cushions, pillowcases or upholstery. At the other extreme, a small wallpaper pattern won't make a small room bigger but can make you feel dizzy, so use it on just one wall and paint the others in a harmonising colour.

## creating an aura

Correlate your favourite pattern with your chosen style: stripy florals with grey-green paintwork and gilt detailing for a French boudoir look; paisley and crewelwork with coloured muslin, beading and metallic thread to evoke an Indian theme. For a modern retro style, use a limited amount of dots, circles or spots either as a wall or fabric pattern and fill in with colour and texture choices that underline the theme.

## pattern v. plain

When bold, colourful patterns are used together, include some soothing accents of white, grey, beige or black. In conjunction with single-coloured walls use boldly patterned fabrics generously, but, if the walls are patterned, stick to plain-coloured fabrics. Even a single element of bold pattern – used on a stool cover or bed throw for example – will give a decorative edge to an otherwise plain scheme.

## shape and line

Diagonal pattern such as trellis- or latticework give the illusion of width and height, while vertical and horizontal stripes emphasise height and length respectively (see 49). Pattern can be used discreetly for definition – for example, a Greek key pattern or a simple check (see 49) used as a border can smarten up a plain wood floor or carpet.

## alternative pattern

Pattern is found not just in fabrics and wallpapers but also in stone and wood flooring, in the pattern of a woven chairback or the geometric layout of bricks and tiles. And don't forget the pattern of sunlight through slatted blinds or the shadow shapes on walls created by atmospheric lighting. Ornaments and pictures contribute pattern too.

## pattern tips

Before choosing any pattern, consider the pattern repeat and how a design will look when hung: floral designs are particularly likely to turn out looking like columns (see 50). It's useful to know that a bold design on a lightweight fabric, such as silk or sheer, provides a quite different look to the same pattern on velvet or linen union.

## suiting the en suite

Geometric designs, such as single motif and Islamic shapes with their soothingly repetitive rhythm work well on bathroom tiles. However, the repetitive pattern of tiles is difficult to visualise, so lay out a few sets of tiles to see how they look in a block before buying them. You can also create focused areas of pattern by using mosaic tiles as splashbacks to the basin and bath.

# 47 fabric fantasy

Fabric is fundamental to the comfort of your bedroom but it also conveys style and ambience. We all have our personal likes and dislikes but here are some suggestions for top fabrics that might find favour in your scheme.

## curtains

For winter warmth try velvet, cord or wool felt (see 59), but if your style is light and airy or you want to ring the changes in summer, turn to a silk mix or unlined linen.

## sheers

The drab nylon curtains of yesteryear have thankfully given way to a multitude of delightful sheer fabrics. Plain cotton voile is perfectly acceptable but why not think about the new metallic-shot sheers or sheers with an embossed or woven pattern?

**10 ideas**

## on the walls

Fabric on the walls insulates well and creates a cocooned and cosy bedroom (see 77, 81, 82). Among the best fabrics to use are felt or baize, crewelwork, or toile de Jouy.

## sheets

Egyptian cotton is popular and Irish linen has a unique look and tactile attraction, but for pure sensuality, nothing beats silk satin (see 83).

## pillowcases

Pillowcases to match your sheets are usually a first choice but if you have extra pillows for a luxurious-looking bed, you might contrast-cover them in a fabric used elsewhere in the room (see 83).

## bed covers

Pure Merino wool or mohair blankets are expensive but hard to beat for quality; a less expensive choice is a soft fleece fabric. If you have sheets and blankets, you might need a matelassé cotton figured quilt and could finish the look off with a faux fur or soft fleece.

## bedhead

Contemporary bedheads are more about visual effect than head support (see 81). For tactility there's faux suede fabric, for fashionability, denim, corduroy, tweed or satin, but for practicality make washable linen union slipcovers.

## cushions

Cushions provide an excuse to indulge in a small amount of opulence. Consider mixing faux fur, cashmere and silk, or embroidery, appliqué and dévoré (see 83).

## upholstery

An elegant easy chair, stool or sofa – if you've the room – might be covered in damask or stamped velvet, but for something more edgy, why not try faux animal skin?

## bathroom choice

It's difficult to include luxurious fabrics in an en suite or bathroom in case they rot or stain. Instead, stick to practical, washable fabrics such as cotton and towelling. For a touch of luxurious texture you could include some ribbed or combed-cotton bath sheets.

# 48 special-effect fabrics

Among the myriad fabrics, including the purely decorative and the essentially practical, some stand out as making a special contribution to the bedroom scene. These might be considered for their specific sensual, tactile character because they are a little out of the ordinary or because, even in small quantities, they add to the room's decorative attributes.

• Pinstripe and suit flannel bedcovers and upholstery for a tailored masculine look
• Felt for no-sew curtains hung from poles through over-sized eyelets
• Dévoré or stamped velvet for sensual texture as a bedspread or throw
• Faux fur lined in velvet or suede-effect fabric for a decadently de luxe bedspread
• Permanent-pleat curtains of silk or silk-effect mix for the way it shimmers and hangs without the need for heading tape
• Voile with metallic threadwork lines or patterns to shimmer at the window or use as an alternative bedhead hanging
• Satin for adding a contrast border to anything textural from a bedspread to cushions and curtains
• Cashmere for the softest and most luxurious extra bed cushions
• Burlap or hessian for inexpensive earthy companions to stone, tiles and wood
• Tweed for its novelty, subtle colour range and adaptability to the non-sexist bedroom

# checks and stripes

Among the most easily put together and versatile of combinations, checks and stripes are great for bedrooms.

## exclusive use

If you use stripes and checks on their own, 'anchor' them with areas of solid colour or neutral space somewhere in the bedroom.

## smartening up

For a cosmopolitan bedroom look, use a stripe or check in a smart fabric such as a taffeta, silk or moiré. Stripes and checks are also sophisticated with a decorative trim such as ribbon, fringing, gimp or braid. Pinstripes and checked shirt cottons combine well with other fabrics to create a smartly tailored masculine bedroom.

## simple or complex

Checked pattern can be as simple and monochromatic as gingham or as complex and full of colour as tartan. A complex check used on one wall only will be easy on the eye, especially if any pictures are lined up with the checks.

## little and large

Curtains or blinds in a large check could be lined and bordered with a smaller version. Both stripes and checks can be used to line bed hangings or simply employed unlined as the hangings themselves.

## lining it up

Striped wallpaper makes a good partner to floorboards as the lines echo each other. Striped fabric can also be cut to emphasise the contours of upholstered furnishings and tailored bed dressings. Be very sparing with bright and trendy 'bar-code' stripes for bedroom use – they're fun, but very busy.

## composite stripes

Stripes are also part of more complex designs such as brocade and serpentine floral patterns, which add further pattern dimension and colour. These are most suitable for a classic French- or Italian-orientated scheme.

## scale and stripes

The scale of wall stripes should be judged by their colour contrast and the spatial dimensions involved. The closer and narrower the stripes, the louder the contrast and the more the area they cover will visually close in.

## checking out the bathroom

A bathroom is ideal for using checks and diamonds thanks to the geometric shape of wall and floor tiles. For example, you could create a large chequerboard or diamond pattern in tiles to define the shower or bath area.

# 50 the greatest fabric combos ever

There are certain bedroom partnerships that are destined to go exceedingly well together, if only they can be introduced under the right circumstances and are given a favourable environment. A well-chosen fabric will underscore the bedroom theme and, when one appropriate fabric is used in juxtaposition with another, just as in cooking, the partnership can be sublime. You don't need to employ an interior designer to conjure up delicious fabric mixes, just take your inspiration from the pages of magazines and the offerings below.

## on safari

If you like the natural and tactile attributes of an African interior, adapt them to an urban environment:
• Bed runner and cushions made from African Kente cloth (basket-weave strip cloth with symbolic patterns)
• Indigo blue raw silk square-quilted and tuft-buttoned bedspread
• Natural muslin curtains with a blue-and-black cotton border

## bright and beautiful

Remember that it's not only the fabric alone, but also what you do with it that counts. It's easy to make wool felt interesting with pinking shears and here it accompanies contrasting fabrics of satin and herringbone for a light-hearted but still bedroomy look:
• Lime-green felt curtains with pinked zigzag edges
• Black/grey/green-patterned linen union bedspread
• Grey and black felt and satin cushions with pinked edges
• Herringbone black/white upholstery

## french dressing

For some reason shiny yellow, chocolate and matt grey work fabulously well together. This scheme has a French influence:
• Yellow damask curtains with broad chocolate trim
• Grey velvet bedspread with chocolate satin scalloped border
• Embroidery and linen cushions
• Square-and-flower motif upholstery

## pictures and posies

Toile de Jouy, gingham, roses and lace are classic partners:
• Red toile de Jouy bedspread trimmed with gingham
• Cotton- and lace-trimmed sheets and pillowcases
• Rosebud chintz curtains or blind with contrast green border
• Large check for upholstery

## highland fling

It can be difficult to find fabric combinations that appeal to both partners in the bedroom, but this is one that should:
• Paisley-print bedspread
• Fern green chenille throw
• Tartan taffeta cushions
• Curtains in a striped silk in heather, grey and fern green
• Heather-coloured tweed upholstery, trimmed with leather

# 51

## second-hand rose

The floral motif has long been a popular bedroom choice but today's designs cover a far more versatile spectrum of reference and style, much influenced by innovative fabric technology and production techniques.

• Two or three different floral patterns can be used together but care is needed not to suffocate the room. Plenty of plains will prevent this.

• Some floral and leaf designs suit a masculine bedroom to contrast with purposefully male ingredients such as leather and black lacquer. Examples are abstract monochromatic designs, rich damasks and jacquard woven patterns.

• Use a large, graphic floral pattern as a single wallpapered wall, add a small scale flower design plus a stripe or check. Use these to contrast line or border each other.

• Explore the modern potential of crisp and unfussy floral pattern with sleek furniture, contemporary flooring materials and lots of space.

• Hang light, floral curtains when spring arrives and change them for something darker, heavier and cosier for the winter months.

• Use an all-over floral design on walls, ceiling and curtains or blinds in a small room to create a charmingly cocooned haven.

• Modern chintzes are often produced with an artificially aged finish, which softens the colours and produces a more informal, harmonious effect.

• Note how colour influences the effect of a pattern: a faded pale-pink flower conveys a different mood to a bold purple one.

• You can use the same small floral pattern in different colourways together as long as they are within the same balanced tonal range.

• A large-scale life-like botanical print is best shown off as a flat window or wall panel. If the window is wider than the fabric, add a contrast fabric border.

# keep it practical 52

Certain fabrics are special to the bedroom because their unique, practical qualities and specific in-bedroom contribution elevate them above others which rely on fashion, whim or budget.

## cotton

Cotton comes in different weights, textures and colours. It's tough and resilient and combines well with other fabrics. It is also anti-static and cool to sleep in: Egyptian cotton is a top-quality choice for bed sheets. Although it might need more vigorous ironing than cotton-mix sheeting, it washes, wears and feels better. For a luxurious bath sheet, cotton terry towelling has an uncut loop pile for a thicker, more comforting and more absorbent towel.

## linen

Linen has a unique touch and texture and is sometimes mixed with cotton to increase its suppleness. It ages well and comes in a great range of subtle colours and designs. It combines easily with other fabrics and can be used for curtains, bed dressing, upholstery or loose covers.

## silk

Silk is the finest, smoothest and strongest natural fibre. It takes dye well and comes in a wide range of exceptionally beautiful colours. It isn't susceptible to mildew, nor will dry cleaning damage it. However, in time, strong sunlight will make it fade and deteriorate so it is best located away from bright light. Even in a small quantity, such as for cushions or a wall panel, it adds eye-catching quality.

## fleece

Although this is a synthetic fabric, its qualities of warmth and softness make it practical and comforting as blankets, throws and cushions. Also, it comes in a good range of bright and subtle colours – and is inexpensive too.

## felt

Felt doesn't fray and so it may be left unhemmed and can be simply cut and shaped as required. Its structural quality makes an unusual curtain fabric and looks both smart and tactile when used for upholstery and cushions.

# 53 make light work of lighting

A well-planned lighting system will highlight the bedroom's decorative assets, will be practical and will help create the desired mood. The three types of lighting you will need are background, task and accent lighting. Especially in a bedroom, the secret of success is flexibility so you can switch instantly from bright and functional to moodily atmospheric. Using today's sophisticated systems and cutting-edge design, bedroom illumination can be subtle and atmospheric or sensationally decorative according to your needs.

## getting enough

It's wise to install more lighting than you think you'll need, wiring the various types to different dimmer switches. Darker-coloured rooms need extra lighting because dark colour absorbs light, particularly if the walls are a matt finish.

## lighting to wash by

This is a plea for atmospheric lighting in the bathroom. Naturally, there must be practical lighting too, but the bathroom should be a relaxing, self-indulgent retreat with two independent types of lighting: one practical, the other atmospheric.

## the right bulb

Tungsten bulbs, the regular creamy yellow filament light bulbs, are sometimes tinted for mood effect. Halogen lights are either low- or mains voltage and provide a whiter, crisper light. Their sparkle makes them good as uplights, downlights, spots and for accent lighting. Fluorescent tubes emit a hard light unless they are installed behind a special opaque baffle, which will act to soften the glare.

## natural light

Strong natural light is more invigorating and beneficial than artificial light. Sunlight can be exploited by clearing the window area as much as possible and positioning furniture so that the natural light can be enjoyed while getting up or relaxing in the evening. If your natural light is poor, create a warm, inward-looking atmosphere with dark colours and lots of adaptable electric lighting.

## lightly balanced

It's important to minimise areas of harsh shadow in the bedroom as they disturb the visual flow and create a sense

of unease. Lighting distributed evenly around the room at different levels will help prevent this.

## getting in the mood

The more flexible and user-friendly the lighting control system, the easier it will be to create atmosphere on demand: switches with dimmers should be placed by the door and at either side of the bed. Don't forget candlelight – for its scent as well as romance.

## seeing the light

Requirements for bedroom task lighting are for reading, working, applying and removing make-up and for seeing into wardrobes and cupboards.

## in the background

In a bedroom, background or ambient lighting is the least used, its main function being to smooth out harsh angles and shadows. If you choose a central ceiling light, do so for the decorative, rather than practical, contribution it will make to the room.

## different accents

Fixed accent lighting reduces the flexibility you have for changing the bedroom's layout or the way you have arranged pictures and ornaments. You should of course provide accent lighting for display shelves that are permanent, but freestanding lights or clip-ons will be more versatile.

## checking positions

The positioning of lights can be manipulated to eliminate hard shadows and glare. Before you make any final decisions, how about checking what the lights will look like from the lying-on-the-bed perspective?

## 54 lighten up

For comfortable, unobtrusive illumination that eliminates shadows in the bedroom, background lighting needs to spread the light broadly downwards and upwards. Use separate dimmer switches to give control over the individual elements.

### ceiling lights

A single pendant light can create a bland or glaringly unflattering light and should only be considered when its decorative benefit exceeds its lighting contribution.

### five ceiling lights to suit

1 • The classic paper lantern, appropriate for a minimalist or Zen bedroom
2 • A pendant chandelier
3 • The star lantern for an ethnic-styled bedroom
4 • Abstract sculptural shapes associated with contemporary interiors
5 • A multi-branched 'Octopus' light to suit a retro bedroom look.

### brackets or sconces

Candlelight brackets or sconces are a source of soft ambient light and elegance, especially in pairs flanking a handsome mirror.

### wall washers and floor lights

Low-level uplights create a soothing environment, will enhance the texture of the wall and will highlight architectural detail.

### downlights

Small downlights in the ceiling provide even background light. They look dramatic fitted around the perimeter of the room only and linked to dimmer switches.

### lamps

Well-placed table and floor lamps at different heights and linked to dimmer switches create the most balanced and harmonious background lighting. The light can be manipulated by choosing lampshades with reflective coloured linings: gold, for instance, will ensure a warm radiance. Shades and bases need to be carefully matched for style and size.

## 55 practical lighting

Practical bedroom lighting can be achieved either by installing discreet fittings when you build the room or by having add-on light fittings that reflect the bedroom style.

### reading lights

A bedside light should be high enough to throw light onto a book without causing any glare.Space-saving designs include wall-mounted reading lights on swivel arms or, if you are commissioning an over-sized bedhead, have the lighting incorporated in it. An angle-poise floor lamp is versatile as it could be moved to provide task lighting in another area of the room.

### vanity lighting

Lights on either side of the dressing table or wall-mounted mirror provide even, glare-free illumination but you could also place your dressing table so natural light will fall on your face. You'll need adequate light for all that time in front of the long mirror, too!

## cupboard lighting

Lighting that comes on automatically when you open a cupboard is very convenient, while lighting behind opaque door panels reduces the visual bulk of a large area of cupboards.

## work lighting

A single halogen desk lamp with a pivoting arm is adequate for a small work area. If you have shelves above your work area, you could install small downlights behind a lip in the bottom shelf.

## lighting an en suite

Mirror lights are most efficient either side of the mirror. Halogen downlights provide sparkling crisp light: position them so you can read in the bath. As an extra, atmospheric light can be provided by lights set behind glass bricks in the wall or behind custom-designed baffles, and if you have the room, don't forget groups of small candles on the ledge around the bath.

# 56 display lighting

Accent or display lighting creates directional highlights that illuminate objects, pictures, an interesting architectural detail or a piece of furniture. They add another layer to the bedroom lighting environment.

## uplights

Miniature uplights hidden in lipped shelving units will discreetly illuminate decorative items. Larger uplights can be placed at floor level in front or behind objects to dramatic effect. This method of lighting also has the advantage of eliminating any dark corners in the room.

## downlights

Swivel downlights with a narrow beam partially recessed into the ceiling direct light onto a particular area or object. Alternatively, they can be attached to the underside of a shelf and concealed by a lip.

## spotlights

To illuminate a single item a clip-on or lamp-stand spotlight will give mobility and variable control. Most modern spotlights take incandescent reflector bulbs with silver interiors or low-voltage halogen bulbs with integrated reflectors to project light and disperse heat backwards.

## track lighting

For a studio bedroom, track lighting, with individual lamps that can focus on specific areas provides a degree of versatility. It can be 'floated' in a high-ceilinged area without interfering with the visual flow because it runs on unobtrusive thin wires.

## picture lights

If you have a special work of art to draw attention to, you can illuminate it with an integrated picture light, but note that this works best with unglazed pictures as there can be glare from the reflection. However, an integrated picture light means you are committed to a certain lighting position. An alternative is a miniature ceiling-mounted picture light with a focused beam that fits the object precisely, but these are expensive.

# invasion of privacy what to do with your windows

Privacy needs in the bedroom go further than merely shielding our private lives from the neighbour opposite! We also need to consider privacy in relation to sex, washing, toilet and dressing, and if street lighting or daylight disturb your sleep, you may want to block out all the light.

## taking shape

Sometimes a bedroom scheme is driven by a window's style. For example, a dormer window doesn't lend itself to a Zen-style scheme, and panoramic floor-to-ceiling windows don't conjure up a Nordic-inspired bedroom. In such cases, you may have to go for a scheme that incorporates the window's idiosyncrasies.

With a neutral window, you can match the window treatment to your decorative theme. A pelmet and curtains that pool onto the floor suit a boudoir-style room, while an oriental-themed bedroom might have fine linen blinds. Floral curtains hung from a pole with bow ties and lace under-curtains partner an utterly feminine bedroom.

**5 ideas**

## sheer folly

Curtain sheers alone allow you to look out on the world during the day without being seen, but the effect will be reversed at night (see 48). A roller blind behind the curtains will serve for night-time privacy in this situation.

## lining benefits

Naturally, the thicker the curtain material, the more light it will exclude, but to optimise light and sound exclusion curtains can be interlined and lined with light-blocking material. There are also blinds with a special backing treatment that cuts out light. An alternative is a blind made from one of the variety of light-restricting materials such as a dark, heavy fabric, suede- and leather-effect fabric, aluminium or wood.

## on valance

Valances can be girly and beguiling in feminine, floral bedrooms and work particularly well with lightweight fabrics and sheers. They can also be paired with a shaped pelmet board to add a soft outline to the window.

## changing perspectives

To add height to the bedroom, fix a fabric valance, pelmet, or up-stand well above the top of the window architrave so that the curtain drop is extended; to visually broaden a window, hang your curtains well outside the window frame. In a bedroom where you wish to maximise the sense of space, allow the curtains to fall in straight folds to the floor. This will extend the vertical dimension and help maintain visual continuity.

# 58 window dressing

It's very easy to get carried away with the aesthetic enjoyment of beautiful curtain fabrics and trimmings or innovative alternative window treatments, but the priorities for bedroom window dressing should be more practical.

• When making your own curtains from washable fabric, allow extra length for shrinkage or pre-wash the fabric.

• Having fallen for an expensive curtain fabric or sheer, buy just enough to make a single panel to hang straight to the floor, adding a border on either side to make up the window width if necessary. This especially suits contemporary large-scale floral or photoprint designs as you can see the whole motif.

• For an unobstructed view from the window combined with privacy, take 'half-measures'. Try hanging 'café' curtains across the lower half of the window or installing half shutters.

• Lining curtains with a tiny motif-printed cotton, gingham or ticking fabric provides an attractive view of the curtains that can be enjoyed by people looking in from the outside.

• If your curtain headings are going to be on view, contrast-bind them for a smartly defined finish.

• Personalise ready-made curtains by adding borders, trims, appliqué, ribbon or buttons or enliven a plain bought blind with appliqué, stencils or a stick-on ribbon border.

• For unusual tiebacks, think wire, jute, leather or even a pair of decorative belts.

# 59 heavy curtains run for cover

Heavy curtains are cosy – good for cold winter nights and bad views. They also insulate against light, sound and pollution. Velvet, wool mixes, linen and corduroy are substantial fabrics, while silk, taffeta and chintz are ideal for a lighter, romantic style. Whatever fabric you choose, heavy curtains will eat up a large chunk of your budget and you really won't want to change them again for a while, so think long-term adaptable rather than this year's fad.

## something different

• Unlined wool felt hangs in concertina folds from giant metal eyelets
• Checked woollen blankets with frayed edges finished with grosgrain ribbon
• Antique quilts; if one isn't big enough use two, cut and sewn in alternate strips
• Waffle cotton bedspreads with tab tops
• Dress or suit fabrics (narrower than curtain fabric). Try herringbone or hounds-tooth check, lined with shirting fabric for a masculine look. For a more feminine version, use a knobbly bouclé in lavender or heather pink edged with moiré silk.

# sheer excitement

With a range of revolutionary fabrics, superb colours and adventurous weaves, unlined lightweight window curtains are very much back in fashion – so start that curtain-twitching now!

The beauty of sheers is in the fabric, rather than the heading. Gathered tape headings on hooks are the simplest, ruched headings provide a pocket to slot a pole or wire through or can be used to give a frill above the pole, while knife pleats and pin-tucked headings are more elaborate alternatives. Or you could simply tie the sheer to a pole or dowelling with satin ribbons.

Sheers don't need fancy or heavy-duty fixings, either. You have the choice of ties, tabs, hooks, rings, pincer clips or eyelets used with plastic-coated wire or tension wire, or with metal, Perspex or wooden poles.

## sheer style

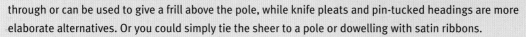

- Some weaves are loose or delicately worked and make a change from pure white sheers. For contrast, you could add a border of slinky satin silk or velvet.
- 'Parachute' silk and linen make fine partners when they're sewn together in horizontal bands with drawn thread-work ribbon between them to allow maximum fluidity. Suspend from tension wire through eyelets.
- Brighten up lengths of plain sheer fabric with appliqué: use scraps of contrasting fabrics in cut-out shapes of stylised leaves or flowers, circles or squares; or apply pockets of the main fabric to hold a changing exhibition of natural objects such as feathers, crystals, shells, dried leaves.
- The intricate work of timeless antique lace is best shown off as a flat panel rather than in gathered folds.
- Plan your night-time lighting to highlight metallic threads in a sheer fabric to give you daytime and night-time benefit (see 56).
- A system of sliding fabric panels on floor tracks or in the window frame can be opened or closed depending on the need for privacy and light. A patterned, coloured sheer with some weight is best, or you could use a combination of transparent and opaque fabric.

# blind alley

## 61

As full-and-fancy curtain styles lose popularity, window blinds have become increasingly vogueish. They suit today's pared-down interior schemes and – let's be honest – save on expensive fabric.

• A roller blind is the most simple and useful of all, in stiffened or laminated fabric or in a firm fabric.

• Inverted roller blinds ensure privacy without excluding all the light or view. The blind pulls up from a 'cassette' box fixed to the sill or outside the window recess.

• A Roman blind folds into flat pleats by means of cords. They look rather clean, smart and minimal and come in all sorts of materials from opaque or translucent fabrics to faux leather and suede.

• A Swedish blind with the cord gliding through glass rings attached to the batten heading works best with a naturally heavy fabric like linen.

• A reverse blind has a pair of cords and architrave-mounted screw-eyes. It rolls up from the bottom. It suits lightweight fabrics best.

• A Venetian or louvered blind is a sleek and modern solution for a window that doesn't require any dressing up. It can be made of stiffened fabric, wood, and perforated or solid aluminium.

• Vertical blinds suit floor-to-ceiling situations. They are made from synthetic polyester fabrics or plain or perforated aluminium.

• Inexpensive pinoleum blinds consist of thin pieces of wood bound with cotton, which usually roll up and are held in place with cords. They come in many colours, or can be natural or varnished.

• Bamboo blinds are light and textural with a natural finish.

• Paper blinds are inexpensive. They work well in a Zen scheme and could be used to create zones in the bedroom in place of sliding screens.

# 62 alternative cover

There are situations where a different method of covering the window is needed, either because the shape of the window requires it or your bedroom style suits a particular look. But you don't need an excuse; you might just like one of them!

• Plantation shutters, or California shutters, are versatile and stylish. They look smart on their own, or can be combined with dress curtains. The wooden slats open and close with a push-rod, or another type has hinged flaps allowing just the lower or upper half of the window to be shuttered.

• Sliding panels fixed to the ceiling are a neat solution to screening large areas of window – and for dividing the bedroom into zones (see 31, 32). When pulled by a draw rod, the linked panels slide behind one another.

• Hinged portière rods work well on tall, awkwardly placed windows. They allow panels of fabric to be swung open or closed.

• A freestanding screen (see 94) is an alternative for covering a bathroom or bedroom window, though it's unlikely to cover the entire window. If you have a fabric-covered screen, use two different fabrics on either side for versatility.

# combination treatments

Layering curtains, sheers and blinds can be both practical and decorative. It allows you to introduce different textures, pattern and colour or play down a busy main curtain pattern with a cool, plain underlayer. On the practical side, a blind or sheer will give some privacy when the heavy curtains are open. If the main curtain fabric is a sheer, it could be partnered by a blind or second layer of curtains to exclude the outside world.

## doubled-up

A bedroom looks cosy and well dressed with dress curtains combined with an ethereal sheer fabric. Use a special double cord-and-track system, or, if the sheer is to remain static, hang it from a rod and tension wire.

## loop the loop

If your window has a lovely outline, preserve it while providing some degree of privacy. Make a luxurious fabric with a mitred border of a heavier fabric into a simple flat panel. To hold it back, hook it high from a loop on the opposite wall.

Add a roller blind, perhaps with a border of the same fabric as the panel.

## textural effects

Double curtains or combinations of blinds and curtains maximise the potential for big textural contrasts (see 44). Bamboo or straw blinds can be paired with a lustrous woven fabric or with a sleek delicate silk or taffeta edged with linen or hessian. Alternatively, the roles can be reversed using a fine linen or open-weave fabric for the blind and chunky earthy burlap or tweed for the curtains.

# 64
# problem windows

It's ironic that a problem window often has an interesting shape and so really looks best without any adornment, but for practical reasons you may want to cover it up at night.

• If you have floor-to-ceiling panoramic windows your options are sliding screens, vertical Venetian blinds or concertina-style blinds.

• A bay or bow window is awkward to curtain; the best solution is to use a series of blinds. Alternatively, have curtains made to fit each window or hang fixed curtains either side.

• An arched window is such a bonus that it would be a shame to cover it, but you can make a Roman blind with a shaped-to-fit mdf

insert or use made-to-measure shutters.

• Options for a dormer window include a roller- or Roman blind, or hinged portière rods with short curtains that can be swung back against the interior window reveal. Any of these is preferable to standard short curtains.

• Skylights pose a particular problem. There are specially designed Venetian or mini-blinds that draw along the window frame.

• Round or 'ox-eye' windows are usually left uncovered but, for the sake of a good night's sleep, you could add a simple black-out curtain which can be drawn right back leaving the window clear for day time.

• A window that abuts a wall can't take a pair of curtains. A single curtain or a blind will cover it.

# 65

# tracks and fittings

All drawing curtains have to be suspended from poles, rods, wires or tracks. Give some thought to how the headings and method of hanging all work together, taking into account the weight and style of material, the decorative style of your bedroom and the outlook and dimensions of your windows.

• Tension wire with rings and eyelets or with curtain clips is a neat, minimalist option for sheers, lightweight curtains and room dividers.

• Fixed headings for curtains, sheers and blinds can be attached to a narrow batten or board fixed on or above the window architrave.

• Tracks are usually made of metal or plastic and can be corded or uncorded. Some are designed for curtains and valances together, others can take two sets of curtains. Some are made specially for a bay or bow window. Conceal plastic curtain track behind a fascia board or pelmet, or at least disguise it with fabric or decorative tape.

• Wooden poles with knobs and finials come in a variety of sizes and are usually associated with heavy curtains. They can be stained, painted or even covered in the curtain material. Internally tracked and corded wooden poles are also available.

• Metal poles and rods are made in a variety of finishes such as iron, brass and chrome.

• Perspex poles are particularly suitable for hanging delicate or sheer fabrics.

• Expansion poles are a neat solution for recessed windows or for any window where it's difficult to fix any other curtain fitting. Although they can't support heavy curtains, they're excellent for sheers and panels.

• An ever-increasing number of innovative blind and curtain fixings are available. You can now choose from a range of rings and clips, huge metal eyelets or simple cased or tab tops.

# don't be floored by flooring

We're spoilt for bedroom flooring options these days, aren't we? Goodbye to the scruffy cord tile or shocking (literally) nylon carpet and worn bedside rug and welcome to a fabulous range of updated classics and new-look designs, as well as cutting-edge hard flooring materials. There has been a huge surge of interest in all sorts of hardwood and laminate floors to suit the leaner bedroom look, tiles and natural stone have always had a place in bedroom design according to country and style, while carpet is undergoing a major design revival. Old favourites such as lino and cork, which were once associated with the kitchen and bathroom, have been given a timely face-lift and now reappear in glamorous guise to floor the bedroom. Alternatives such as rubber, glass and leather all have their part to play in the new-look bedroom, adding texture, colour and an unadulterated 'wow' factor!

## budget

Your flooring choice will probably be influenced by the length of time you propose to stay in residence: you can't take a fixed floor with you but you could invest in a big rug and cover your inadequacies. Given that a new floor makes a huge visual impact as well as an impact on your wallet, you will want to link what you spend to capital return, aesthetic effect and practicality.

## practicality

Above all, a floor needs to be practical for your individual situation and use. Think beyond the visual effect to wear-and-tear, staining, foot comfort, animals and children. Can you combine your flooring with under-floor heating (see 16)? If you have pets in your bedroom consider the ease of cleaning and hygiene. If you have an in-bedroom bath or shower, you will want to choose a floor that is impervious to damp and water staining.

## continuity

What other flooring do you have in the home? To help the overall visual flow, it's a good idea to have a link between the flooring of the bedroom and the other rooms, particularly if there's an element of open-plan living. Likewise, consider continuing the same floor covering into the en-suite bathroom, if appropriate. Joins between rooms can be neatened with threshold strips.

## style

Associate your flooring finish to your bedroom style if possible. For example, dark or pale wood or bamboo floors work well in a minimalist oriental bedroom; pale or white-painted floorboards are associated with Swedish and East Coast American looks; rubber, leather and lino have an edgy look that suits urban loft living. Fitted carpets introduce pattern, form and texture, while rugs can be specifically placed to add focal emphasis – and comfort underfoot – to certain areas.

## space

When making decisions about flooring, consider its effect on the space: the horizontal surface can be manipulated by colour, line and pattern to visually alter a room's proportions: floorboards, laid lengthwise, will elongate a room; a dark, thick-pile carpet will create a cosy cocoon; a brightly coloured rug will draw attention to a particular area; textured rubber flooring gives a unique surface finish for a bedroom.

## aesthetic

Be cautious! Can you live with the new must-have flooring choice for years? As necessary as it may seem now, today's faddish flooring material could be tomorrow's wallet-ache, especially if it clashes with the new bedroom scheme you'll fancy having in a couple of years' time.

## environment

Certain types of flooring help alleviate allergies and prevent the accumulation of dust and bugs. Flooring that minimises dust in the air and is easy to clean will help the allergy or asthma sufferer. Floors that don't throw up dust and other household detritus and are based on natural materials are thought to be best for the health, and these include lino, tiling, stone and wood.

## acoustics

Unfortunately, any hard flooring material will accentuate acoustic echo to some degree – and watch out for the creaking floorboard! For discretion, comfort, a change of texture and to muffle some noise, include a few rugs.

## weight

Most types of stone and all forms of marble are bulky and heavy. Since most timber floor joists are not strong enough to support a stone floor, this is something you must discuss with the fitters. It may be necessary to strengthen the joists if you're dead set on that stone floor.

## en suite

Bathroom fittings should be installed after the lino or vinyl flooring is fitted. It's certainly possible to use fitted carpet (as long as it's not rubber-backed) in an en-suite bathroom but, although it may decoratively unite the bedroom and bathroom, it won't be as practical, long-lasting or as striking visually as floor tiles.

# 67 carpet

There are now many handsome carpet collections so wall-to-wall carpet is making something of a comeback. When choosing, first consider colour, then texture, then whether you want plain or patterned, and finally fibre and weave. Don't dismiss patterned carpet. There are many discreet or fun designs, but whatever you choose, be sure you can live with it for years to come, because carpet is a long-term investment.

## wool

Best-quality carpet has a high wool content, which makes it durable, soft and dirt-repellent. In a bedroom, durability is not such an issue, so an all-wool carpet is ideal. The two main types of pile are twist and velvet. The latter is a classic bedroom choice. The short loop pile of Brussels' weave takes pattern very well and is en-suite-friendly because it is tough and stain-resistant. Berber carpets with their dense looped pile in natural colours suit a neutral scheme.

## natural fibres

All of these provide a useful neutral background, but some are not soft enough for bedrooms and the only one suitable for an en suite is rush matting.

Jute is not hardwearing, but is softer than coir or sisal. Sisal is the strongest and hardest-wearing but is difficult to clean. Coir and seagrass are a bit prickly for bedroom use. If you like the appearance of natural fibres but without the disadvantages, consider a wool mixture carpet that imitates the look.

### advantages of carpet
• Softness
• Textural effects
• Creates a sense of spaciousness
• Introduces pattern and colour
• Insulating qualities

### disadvantages of carpet
• Not good for allergy sufferers
• You can't take a fitted carpet with you when you move
• Might compromise design choices when you re-decorate

# 68 wooden floors

Wooden flooring is the modern preference for many rooms. More comfortable underfoot than tiles or stone, it is good for creating a sense of space and coolness.

## antique floorboards

These have a unique patina and character, but are very expensive. Your own boards may be suitable for restoration, but it's hard work.

## solid-wood flooring

This comes in a wide range of options. Ash, beech and maple are the smoothest and palest, black walnut and merbau are dark and rich. High-density woods like oak are best for bathrooms. Treated with oil and wax, they are pretty water-tolerant. Cost is dictated by the width and length of the boards, and the type of wood. A wide English oak plank is twice the cost of pale elm tongue-and-groove.

## hardwoods

Make sure any hardwood you buy comes from a sustainable source. Teak, wenge, mahogany and iroko are all endangered but there are many eco-acceptable alternatives: merbau – a lovely chestnut colour – dillenia as a substitute for rosewood, and dark-coloured kwila – not stained by water so useful in an en suite. Although expensive, parquet makes an attractive bedroom floor but don't use it in wet areas and have it expertly laid.

## softwoods

These include fir, pine and spruce. They must be finished with a sealer and polished. Sheets of sealed and varnished plywood (marine ply for an en suite) are inexpensive and can be given a makeover with paint or stain.

## laminate

Cheaper than solid wood and easy to lay, but not hardwearing, laminate is damaged by high heels and can't be re-sanded. There are also cheap, nearly maintenance-free, strip floors made from high-pressure laminates. Laminate floors warp when wet, so aren't suitable for an en suite.

## bamboo

An excellent eco-friendly alternative to hardwood and less expensive than laminate flooring. Don't use in the bathroom as it will swell when wet.

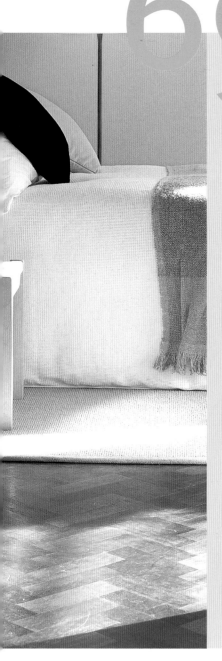

# 69
## rugs and mats

Rugs come in a huge range of designs, colours, textures and patterns and are great for zoning or acting as a focal point.

### the rug choice

• Wool kilims and cotton dhurries are soft and come in rich, mellow colours and many different sizes
• Aubusson-style rugs are a perfect choice for an updated classic French or Italian bedroom scheme
• Antique rugs are great for their character and soft colouring
• Rag rugs are inexpensive and look best on a pale or painted wooden floor
• Shag-pile and flokati rugs are fun and are a real bedside treat-for-the-feet
• Animal-skin-effect rugs lend an exotic note to an earthy neutral scheme or will associate handsomely with an updated Art Deco look
• Real animal hides add texture and 'edge' to a hard floor
• Tatami mats and Goza mats suit a Zen-styled room
• Natural-fibre mats can be bought with lovely borders that soften their effect

# 70
## other types of flooring

Sometimes carpets, wood or rugs just don't make the grade. If you want bedroom flooring with attitude, consider one of these unusual options.

• Rubber tiles and sheeting are the flooring of the moment! They are anti-slip (not non-slip), anti-static, noise absorbing, are warm underfoot and resistant to burns. They can imitate stone and come in a range of smooth or textured effects in many different colours.
• Linoleum, in sheets or tiles and made from natural materials has made a big comeback. Hygienic and eco-friendly, it comes in many designs and colours, including textured finishes such as 'crocodile' and 'tweed'.
• Vinyl flooring, made from PVC, comes in sheets or tiles that can be laid over almost any existing hard surface. It is not as long lasting or easy to maintain as lino, but is usually less expensive. Look out for innovative vinyl-faced cork tiles printed with photographic images. They look great in an en suite.
• Cork is back! Now in subtle new colours, it's durable, soft, impervious to water, a good insulator and eco-friendly.

• Leather floor tiles are luxurious, warm, sensuous and sound insulating. However, they should be protected from direct sunlight, excessive heat and sharp objects – including high heels!

• Concrete is an unusual bedroom flooring choice but is great if you want a raw and handsome look. It can be coloured, skimmed with screed for a suede-like texture or finished with a shiny resin coat.

• Consisting of marble chips set in a cement base and polished to a high sheen, terrazzo makes a handsome and non-slip floor.

• Tiles offer a wide choice, from unglazed terracotta, to glazed ceramic. They are good for continuity with an en suite or wet room, but not if you want cosy bare feet! Make sure you choose non-slip and check for weight (see 66) and sub-floor requirements.

• Stone is another luxurious bedroom flooring option. Choose from cool limestone or marble for classic good looks (honed marble mosaic or tesserae are best for an en suite because they are non-slip), granite or slate for more rugged appeal. Not all are as durable as you might think, though, so check before buying. And of course their weight and sub-floor requirements are an issue.

• For the cutting-edge interior how about glass floor tiles? They come in a range of colours and are available in a sandblasted non-slip finish.

# give your floor a treat

### time to strip

Although it's messy, stripping old floorboards gives you the look of plain boards without having to buy new. Once they're sanded, stain or paint, then seal with varnish.

### top coat

All solid wood floors (see 68) should be sealed to protect them from damp and surface damage. Avoid polyurethane sealants because they are an irritant and will yellow the wood. Instead choose water-based acrylic or an organic treatment such as tung- or citrus-oil. These aren't as hardwearing, so the floor will need regular waxing.

### add an edge

Treat a plain wooden floor to a border such as a Greek key or chequerboard design, or use a stencil for more complexity.

### carpet care

Professional on-site carpet cleaning will help restore your carpet to its former glory. Professionals will comb the pile, power vacuum, machine clean and hand-clean difficult areas. It really is worth the cost.

### skin deep

Clean leather flooring with a lightly damp cloth or mop. Regular bees-wax polishing will keep gaps filled in and improve lustre.

# 72 wall tips

You can be as choosy, opinionated and selfish as you like in the privacy of your bedroom when it comes to deciding on your wall decoration. Whether you want an easy backdrop or a focused style, paint, wallpaper and fabric are the main options while tiles are the most popular en-suite choice.

## in character

Decorate your walls to underline your theme. For example, play up the decorative statement with a dramatic finish, such as a woven bamboo paper in an oriental-style room, or use subtly coloured painted walls to create a neutral backdrop in a soothing bedroom full of textural detail.

## versatility

Your wall treatment can refer to the style of bed and way it is dressed or it could co-ordinate with a curtain colour. Because bedroom wall coverings don't have to be so hard-wearing you could choose a hand-painted paper, suede-effect paint or silk fabric without fear of damage from sticky fingers, muddy dogs or sharp shopping bags!

## disguise

Wallpaper or fabric disguises uneven or architecturally awkward walls. Cross-hung lining paper will smooth rough surfaces and battens will hold fabric away from the walls. A broken paint finish will camouflage an uneven surface better than a solid one.

## get focused

A single dynamically papered wall is enough to illustrate your stylistic direction without overwhelming a small bedroom. For example, convey an oriental flavour with a Chinese-style paper or use a bold flower-and-stripe paper as a background for a pretty boudoir.

## balance and proportion

As the walls are the largest surface in the bedroom, how you decorate them is fundamental to creating the right atmosphere. Clever use of pattern, colour and texture on the walls can make the room look larger or smaller and give visual focus, but balance between these elements is vital to provide a tranquil environment. And remember, daylight has a great effect on how we see colour and texture but in the bedroom, night-time lighting is by far the most important influence.

## architectural details

Dado rails and panels can be a boon or a bore. A high-ceilinged bedroom can accommodate the horizontal divide that a dado rail creates, but in most bedrooms it simply creates bad proportions and affects the visual flow. If the feature is genuine, then it will almost certainly look right and, like other genuine architectural features, should be treasured and enhanced.

## combination finishes

With such a large area to play with, walls offer many opportunities for exciting

combinations. For greatest impact, try to exaggerate the textural differences – a large patterned wallpaper with sleek satin-varnished paint finish; a natural grass-fibre paper with one lacquer-effect painted wall; 'suede' walls with quilted silk wall panels.

## and not forgetting the ceiling

Until the 1920s, the ceiling was considered part of the decorative playground, but it has since been largely ignored. Instead of painting it plain old white, why not adorn it with another colour, with stencilling, geometric shapes or a mural? After all, you spend a third of your life facing the ceiling!

## en-suite specials

Create continuity and a feeling of spaciousness between the bedroom and the en suite by using a single walling material in a neutral colour for the two rooms. Or link the en-suite walls and those of the bedroom following the style of decoration of the bedroom. For instance, use high-gloss tiles and chrome with an updated Art Deco theme, colour-washed tongue-and-groove panelling for the seaside look, and handmade tiles, inlaid mirror and earthy pigment colours to accompany a Moroccan-inspired bedroom.

## trying times

Always try out samples of paint or wallpaper on large pieces of board propped up against the different walls of the bedroom to see how light affects them. Bear in mind, too, the effect that electric light (see Balance and Proportion) will have.

# 73

## paint

Paint is inexpensive and versatile. No wonder it's such a popular finish.

### paint basics

Matt water-based emulsion is the easiest, quickest and most inexpensive method of decorating walls and ceilings. Eggshell and satin finishes are good for surfaces that are vulnerable to marking, for painting radiators or for adding subtle contrast to emulsion.

### eco

Water- or acrylic-based alternatives to solvent-based paints are eco-friendly, better for allergies, skin and nose – and dry quicker!

### colour match

Most paint colours can be found commercially but for an inimitable deep and lustrous finish you can create your own colour using powder pigments or universal stainers in an acrylic base, and apply several coats. Finish with an appropriate varnish.

## textural effects

Distemper paint has a charming chalky finish but casein (milk) paint is more water-resistant and durable and doesn't need stripping before repainting like distemper. Delicate sensual suede-effect paint is a possibility in the bedroom and ultra-matt ranges in nature-inspired textures look good, too.

### lacquer

Lacquer paint in red or black suits an oriental bedroom. It needs a completely smooth surface, so is best applied to a small area – a single wall or cupboard front.

### metallic

Metallics used for contrasting detail add a touch of glamour to a bedroom scheme. Glittery and opalescent paints, either on top of emulsion or for added detail, are another option.

### colourwash

Achieve a soft, cloudy effect with tinted colourwashes using either a pva carrier or diluted emulsion. This finish will need a varnish topcoat.

# 74

## wood

Timber has been used for cladding interior walls for centuries, but except where it grows plentifully, it is no longer common, and especially not for bedrooms. However, it adds warmth and texture and can make a valuable contribution to bedroom and en-suite walls. As with wooden flooring, make sure you buy wood from a sustainable source (see 68).

### panelling

This should be made to measure and expertly fitted. Leave unpainted for a handsomely masculine bedroom, paint it cream or soft green for an Arts and Crafts look, or give it a distressed finish in blue green or dusty pink for an 18-century feel.

### tongue-and-groove

This is panelling's country cousin, conjuring up seaside and rustic bedrooms. Use pale colours to keep the effect light: paint or colourwash in the bedroom, paint and varnish in the en suite.

## rough timber

For a rustic country cabin look or for texture in large open-plan bedroom, use old scaffolding planks or railway sleepers cut into thin cladding planks.

## plywood

An effective and economical alternative to panelling, you can use it to cheat by painting panelling lines on it, or you can sometimes buy it with a veneered finish. Installation is best left to a professional.

## bamboo

With its ridged and glossy texture, bamboo makes a dramatic wall cladding, but it is best confined to a single wall. It is also available as strip-woven wall tiles.

## special treatment

If wood seems too heavy, lighten its effect and emphasise the grain with a colourwash or lime it using a special paste. The result is a weathered, aged look. MDF, chipboard or hardboard can be painted or 'grained' to simulate planking or panelling. A wall-to-wall 'wood' wardrobe could be created in this way too.

# stone, brick, plaster and concrete

Using these wall finishes takes courage and probably a pretty unique bedroom. But they can work well combined with more usual wall treatments. It's best to think extremes – a rough stone wall behind a velvet headboard, a concrete half-wall screening off a glass-and-chrome shower unit, a reclaimed brick wall showing off a gallery of colourful pictures in old gilt frames.

## stone

• Stone is textural, cool, heavy and amplifies sound.

• If you have stone walls, they can be exposed to make a feature wall in the bedroom. In an en suite or shower area, they give the feeling that you are bathing outdoors.

• Limestone and slate can be used on walls and floors so can bring a sense of unity to an en suite or wet room. Marble's opulent image has detracted somewhat from its merits recently, but it is worth considering for its beautiful patterning and colour for en-suite walls. It is slippery when wet, so not recommended for the floor.

## brick

• Brick can suit either a rustic or a contemporary bedroom.

• It comes in a variety of natural shades which you'll have to consider carefully when choosing other colours to go with it in the bedroom

• Interior brick should be treated with sealant to prevent dusting and it can be coloured with masonry paint.

# plaster

• Most walls are finished with plaster or plasterboard, so why not make it into a decorative asset? It gives a softly textured, informal wall finish and works very well on uneven walls.

• Colour pigments may be worked into the dry plaster mix or rubbed into the wall surface. Unpainted plaster must be sealed to stop it dusting. It can be waxed and polished for a deep luminous finish.

• Unfinished plaster should not be used in damp areas, but waterproofed and sound-insulating plasterboard is available.

# concrete

• Concrete's utilitarian appeal isn't for everyone's bedroom, but you could consider using it as a room divider if your bedroom is big enough.

• In the en suite, concrete provides a bold contrast to polished, shiny chrome and porcelain.

# 76 wallpaper

Because patterned walls have been out of fashion for a while, wallpaper has taken a back seat, but if you want to convey a specific decorative image in your bedroom, then wallpaper is the preferred choice. You might choose a warm-coloured dense pattern to create a cocooning environment, a themed design that reflects the style of the room – floral, Provençal, geometric retro, or an extravagantly expensive paper to make a fabulous stand-alone statement. If adding texture is your main aim, go for imitation rice paper or parchment for a Zen den, natural fibre papers as a subtle backdrop to a neutral scheme or imitation suede embossed with a geometric pattern for the retro look.

Innovative wallpapers include those with metallic threads or overlaid abstract metallic shapes. They look stunning under subtle night-time lighting, which is all-important to a bedroom. Papers for en-suite walls are more limited because they have to have a vinyl finish to protect them from moisture, but they make a worthy alternative to tiles and natural claddings where economy is a major consideration.

## practical pointers

• Make sure you take the repeat of a pattern into account when calculating wallpaper quantities. This is especially important with a large design.

• Always look at a picture of the wallpaper hung in situ; it may have an unexpected striped, diagonal, curved or wavy pattern.

• If the walls are uneven or you're using a delicate wallpaper, first line the walls using plain lining paper hung horizontally. You can also use lining paper on the ceiling .

• To make a room appear longer, instead of painting horizontal stripes you could use a broad-striped paper hung horizontally – it's much easier than trying to get your painted lines straight!

• Awkward shapes and angles in a room can be disguised by using a paper with a loose, unstructured pattern on all the surfaces, including the ceiling.

• If you like the idea of fabric on the walls, look for paper-backed fabric. This is much easier to hang than having to batten the walls for fabric.

• Use panels of paper to freshen up cupboard doors, frame them with beading and insert a pretty wallpaper panel or cover them completely with wallpaper if you want them to 'disappear'.

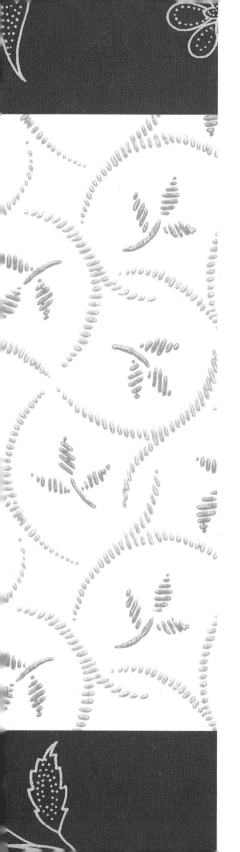

# there is an alternative
## other wall coverings

Even if you are using wallpaper and paint as the main wall treatments in your bedroom, there might be situations where you want to introduce a change of texture, manipulate the light or use a single wall area in an interesting way. Some of these alternatives can be used as a means of refreshing an existing scheme or giving your new style an unexpected dimension.

## glass

There are glass finishes to suit every purpose – sandblasted, etched, printed, textured, toughened, wired and laminated – and in colours to suit every colour scheme. Glass blocks or bricks allow the passage of light and are a fashionable choice, either as en-suite walling or as a dividing wall between bedroom and wet room.

## mirror

A mirrored wall will dramatically enlarge the sense of space in a small en suite, however, it needs to be kept spotless to look good! In the bedroom, where large areas of mirror can be intimidating, it's best used in panels, or divided with beading or trellis. You might front a wall of built-in cupboards with mirror.

## fabric

For loose drapes, hang supple fabric from hooks or brackets so that it falls in swags against the wall, looping from hook to hook. For a tented effect use a striped fabric or light canvas and 'tent' the ceiling too. For ultimate cocooning, fix battens to the walls and staple on lengths of fabric, finishing the joins with braid, gimp or ribbon.

## oddball paper

Tissue paper, wrapping paper, parcel paper and rice paper all make interesting alternative wall coverings. The wall beneath will show through so paint it an appropriate colour. Protect the paper with varnish or a tinted emulsion wash. Use metallic-leaf, too, for a unique burnished tile effect.

# 78 bedtime at last

A bed is a major investment and is often the centrepiece for your bedroom style. Some people choose a bed for its looks while others choose one they hope will ease their back pain. If your bedroom has limited storage space, you might be drawn to a bed with storage potential, or you may decide that your top priority is a really huge bed. But whatever style choice you go for, the first priority is to buy the best mattress you can afford (see 80). Choosing the frame is the next step. The range of prices, styles and qualities of beds and mattresses is enormous. It's enough to make you want to lie down!

## did you know?

Did you know that you spend one-third of your life in bed and that you should replace your mattress every 10 years?

## 10 ideas

## headboards

Most people like a headboard for comfort and to protect the wall behind the bed. You can buy your bed complete with a headboard, or choose a separate one. A traditional upholstered headboard can be finished to match or contrast with your bed dressing or curtains. Modern versions are sometimes just made of wood or consist of a flat, padded surface in a material such as faux suede, moleskin, or even leather. If you are thinking of having a headboard made, order the biggest you can accommodate – bigger is almost always better.

## size matters

An antique or continental bed is often shorter and a different width to a modern standard bed. However, a specialist manufacturer can produce a mattress made to exactly the right dimensions – but this will obviously cost more than a mass-produced one. If you're buying an antique bed, check that the base of the bed is strong and complete, too!

## futons

A futon mattress is ideal for a Zen-style bedroom, but because it lies close to the ground, dust and draughts can be a problem.

## sofa beds

Try it out before buying it; the 'sofa' part can be deceptively commodious and comfortable compared to the 'bed' part! An easily adapted futon-style sofa bed makes a sleek modern alternative.

## daybeds

A daybed with scrolled or comfortably upholstered ends is an elegant option for single occupancy in a studio or loft room where space is limited. Some have a sliding frame underneath containing a mattress so they turn into a double bed when required (see 93).

## well adjusted

Adjustable beds are either manually or electrically operated and give you the option of individualised sitting and sleeping positions. They come with either flexible laminated slats or fully upholstered sections with special mattresses. The ultimate luxury bed has a fully electronically adjustable system, including integrated heating and airing facilities!

## space-savers

Raising your bed on a platform gives the illusion of more space and offers the potential for extra storage underneath, too. Always invest in a good-quality pocket-sprung mattress on top for comfort. For occasional guests, a single bed with another bed underneath that is jacked up to the same height is an option (see 35), or for the ultimate in space-saving, investigate a cupboard bed. This is a complete unit with a spring and hinge mechanism that can be recessed into the wall and lowered into position when required.

## kids' beds

If the children are old enough, bunk beds are an obvious space-saver and fun into the bargain! Avoid claustrophobia by providing good lighting and plenty of headroom. For cosiness, you could surround the beds with curtains or roll-up blinds.

A bed built into a wall cupboard is another fun idea, and space-saving too, while a truckle bed, which pulls out from beneath another bed, is perfectly adequate for sleepovers and keeps little cherub friends close and cosy.

## underbed storage

Many beds have the option of underbed storage. You can buy or order a divan with drawers in the base – either a large drawer at the foot end, a pair of drawers either side or four drawers of varying size. Many low-line modern beds also have underbed storage drawers, while a high bedstead has plenty of space that can be filled with boxes, baskets, zippered cases or drawers on wheels (see 79, 86).

# bed styles

A bed will usually dominate a bedroom, so think before you buy a French antique bed or an ultra-modern chrome bed frame. It will govern the decorations long after you have grown tired of it!

## contemporary wood

Modern wooden bed frames are often on slim, tapered legs or on a low-rise platform, and they sometimes come with a simple headboard or with integral bedside tables. They are ideal for the uncluttered loft or Zen-style bedroom. For luxury and contrast, look for an oversized headboard in tactile leather, suede, woven bamboo or rattan.

## tubular steel

Bed frames of robust tubular steel with an upholstered or wooden headboard make an interesting combination and suit a clean-cut urban bedroom.

## ironwork

A modern take on traditional Italian and Provençal beds, contemporary ironwork beds look more streamlined but still echo the sleek curves of the original.

## divan

The classic divan allows you to have any headboard. It can sit on a slatted or sprung, upholstered base, with or without drawers, can sit on the floor or have short legs. Doubles are usually made in linked sections for manoeuvrability.

## four-poster

The traditional four-poster may seem heavy for today's bedrooms but if you have one, dress it to make the most of it. Modern four-posters are lighter in style with simple uprights. They may be hung with drapes or remain uncurtained. Most are of wood, but some have square-sectioned metal frames.

## lit bateau

The lit bateau or sleigh bed, with its solid wood base and scrolled ends is a classic French design of the early 19th century. It gets its name from its boat or sleigh shape. There are classic and modern interpretations.

## antique beds

Antique beds can either have a metal or a wood – often carved – frame. Some, typically French, versions have canework panels in the head- and footboards, while another has a high, shaped head- and footboard in carved and upholstered wood.

# 80 mattress matters

However glamorous your bed, the mattress is more important. Don't just test it by bouncing up and down on the edge – spend time in the shop lying on it in your usual sleeping and reading positions. And always shop with your partner, as different heights and weights will affect individual comfort.

## sizes

Single: 91cm x 190cm; double: 137cm x 190cm; UK King/USA Queen: 152cm x 198cm (USA 203cmL); UK Superking: 183cm x 198cm; USA King: 193cm x 203cm. Before you buy check the size of doorways and stairwells to make sure the bed will fit! If in doubt, for a double, buy zip-link divans.

## sprung construction

There are three types of sprung mattress: open, continuous and pocket. The number of coils and density of the springs affects the firmness. Many mattresses are 'zoned' for comfort on different body areas and most come in firm-, medium- and soft-support options.

## open springs

The most common type of mattress has rows of hour-glass springs connected by spiral wire and strengthened by a flat or round rod edge. Budget range.

## continuous springs

Made from a single length of wire 'knitted' into interwoven springs linked vertically and horizontally. Has a more responsive feel. Mid- to upper price range.

## pocket springs

Rows of small-diameter springs, each contained in a fabric pocket, giving a high degree of zoned contouring, in varying support options and qualities. Some have a double layer of springs. Mid- to upper price range.

## foam

A good-quality foam mattress should have a density of at least 35kg per cubic metre. They suit slatted bases. The newest are made of visco-elastic foam that moulds itself to the shape of any object or weight but returns to its original state when the weight is removed.

## latex

A good choice for allergy sufferers, it is usually sold with a slatted base but can also be bought with a deep-sprung divan.

## made-to-measure

You can have a mattress made to your requirements or for an antique or unusual bed.

## single solution

Zip-linked divans and mattresses are the answer if you and your partner are different weights and heights or like different degrees of hardness. They are also good if your sleeping patterns are different; you'll each have a degree of independent 'movement'.

## water bed

Although these may conjure up an image of lasciviousness, they are extremely good for poor circulation, bad backs and allergy sufferers.

# look behind you bedhead ideas to suit all tastes

A bedhead, headboard or decorative backdrop provides a 'full stop' to the bed arrangement and adds another element of vertical decoration.

## fabric panel

A length of beautiful fabric (see 47) hung behind the bed gives the illusion and visual definition of a bedhead. Choose a heavy fabric with a non-directional pattern so you can hang it lengthways. Insert a thin batten into a pocketed heading at the top and attach it with rings to hidden hooks on the wall above the bed. Another batten or weights in a hem at the bottom will keep it hanging straight.

## shaggy story

Make an impact with a bedhead made from sheepskin or a flokati rug hung behind the bed or used to upholster an mdf template. Deliciously soft and slightly eccentric!

## reclaimed

A bit of lateral thinking will suggest some interesting 'alternative' bedheads such as carved antique doors, fretwork screens, sanded and painted scaffolding planks and bamboo or rush garden fencing materials.

# 82

## a cut above
# drapes and hangings

You don't have to have a four-poster to dress up your bed with hangings.

### simplicity itself

Twist and drape a length of lightweight or sheer fabric over a large hook in the ceiling or a bracket on the wall above the bed.

### canopy

Four cup hooks fixed to the ceiling above the bed can hold lengths of dowelling parallel with the bed's front edge. Simply drape fabric over the dowelling, allowing the fabric to fall over the front one to form a valance and over the back one to hang down the wall behind the bed.

### pole attachments

An easy drape can be made using two or three poles and finials extending from the wall to hold a throw-over length of material. If you use three poles or bosses, centre the middle one high over the bed to create a triangular, rather than rectangular, shape. Either go for a light and airy effect with a gossamer fabric or give it weight with a contrast lining and border or trimming.

### tester

A tester is a canopy attached to the wall or ceiling above the bed. For a contemporary look simply staple or pin a lightweight fabric to it. A corona has a semi-circular frame. Again, the fabric can be stapled or pinned on but to get even pleating, sew on curtain tape first. A corona works especially well hanging over a daybed.

### alternative dressing

For an updated version of bed drapes on a contemporary four-poster, use soft roll-up fabric blinds or pinoleum or bamboo slatted blinds fixed to the top cross-bars. If you want full curtains, try unusual fabrics such as linen, hessian, taffeta or gingham.

### keeping track

Suspend drapes from ceiling-mounted poles or from tracks carefully lined up with the outline of the bed. A four-poster look without the posts!

# 83 all dressed up

It's important to keep your style perspective focused when it comes to making up the bed: it's all too easy to throw on any old sheets or duvet cover and ruin your carefully thought-out scheme. But first you have to make some basic choices.

## the basics

• A smartly tailored bed needs sheets and blankets: Egyptian cotton sheets are top quality and look and feel crisp and cool, while Irish linen has an inimitable look and softness. Harder work than throwing over the duvet, but blankets in lambswool or ultra-luxurious mohair or cashmere edged with satin offer layers of warmth and tactile pleasure.

• There is always a tussle between the merits of blankets versus duvets. If you choose a duvet look for quality: pocket-stitched goose down is top quality, followed by feather and down and then hollow fibre.

• The best-quality pillows are goose down, followed by duck down and duck feather. There are various grades of synthetic fillings, sizes and shapes.

## the decoration

• A classic quilt or eiderdown offers a warm and comforting top layer for blankets and mixes well with a contemporary style. Today's versions are likely to be made from plain and sumptuous fabrics.

• A bedspread should reflect the decorations of your bedroom. Double-sided versions offer an alternative when they are turned back on the bed or a completely different look when you reverse them.

• A throw or runner adds a touch of modern glamour to a bed.

• When it comes to cushions, mix different shapes and textures but limit the pattern or the bed will look busy rather than inviting. Trimmed and tasselled bolster shapes suit antique French beds, but the tailored version looks at home on a contemporary bed.

### earthy and natural
• linen, burlap, calico, cotton, wool

### tailored and masculine
• herringbone, tweeds, jumbo corduroy, denim

### minimal zen
• printed blue-and-white or black-and-white cotton, a touch of silk

### boudoir
• silky textures, printed florals

### scandinavian
• simple checked and striped cotton

# storage basics

Keeping the bedroom clean and clutter-free will help maintain an organised, harmonious environment, which is fundamental for relaxing and sleeping. The arrangement of bedroom storage needs careful planning so the storage units are chosen for accessibility and efficient use of space. So many different items need to be stored in a bedroom that the result is bound to be a mixture of hanging, drawer and shelf space, in varying proportions. You will also need to consider the size of the storage units and the space allotted to them, and apart from all this, you will have to think about relating your storage to your bedroom style and budget.

**10 ideas**

### distribution

Ensuring that things are easy to put away and retrieve is vital. It will mean you actually use your storage properly. Allocating space for specific items will help enormously.

### suits you?

Choose your storage to suit your lifestyle. If you're a suit person, your cupboard space should be designed with suits and shirts in mind, but if you're a sporty person or have a penchant for expensive underwear you will probably need more shelf and drawer space.

### sharing

If you share your bedroom with someone, you'll also have to share the storage space. This requires some give and take, so allocate space according to need, and stick to it.

### making a fresh start

It's cathartic to sort through your stuff and get rid of what you don't need, but it's essential when planning your bedroom storage. It's easy to find any number of reasons why you must hang onto a certain item of clothing but, if you haven't worn it for more than two years, now is the time to say goodbye!

### keep it moving

Work out how frequently you need to access something, as in 'rarely', 'sometimes' or 'often' and store your possessions accordingly. Just because you have a shoe rack doesn't mean next winter's boots have to occupy valuable space there all the time, so keep things moving.

### walk in

If you are lucky enough to be planning a new en-suite bathroom, build a false wall and you could have a walk-in closet area between the two rooms. If there is little room to open doors, use sliding panels, a neat curtain or a roller blind instead (see 31, 33).

## room to grow

Try and keep some flexibility in your storage arrangements for expansion, change of use or different priorities. Perhaps you could choose a modular system, which can be added to when necessary, or 'building-block' open storage units whose shelf arrangements can be changed as your storage needs change.

## showing off

Are you amazingly tidy, have stunning, colour co-ordinated clothes and iron like a god/goddess? If so, you might opt for open storage or state-of-the-art cupboards with interior lighting so your clothes will be on display – but you'll need a cupboard or chest of drawers for those little things that aren't perhaps so decorative!

## aesthetically pleasing

Exchange those inbred wire hangers with an assortment of wooden ones for skirts, trousers and shirts, line drawers with quality paper, scented if you like – and change it seasonally – and install, and use, shoe racks.

## a good finish

• Hardwood (see 74): cherry, stained oak and walnut for a cosy, dark effect; light oak, maple, ash, beech for a lighter contemporary look
• Softwoods (see 74): waxed and polished or painted; plywood; veneers; mdf (use waterproof for bathrooms) – good for slick urban style
• Bamboo (see 74): textural, aesthetic and original; use either as split lengths or woven 'tiles'
• Glass (see 77): etched or frosted; crisp and contemporary; offers a lighter finish than wood for an entire wall of cupboards, with the possibility of subtle interior lighting
• Polypropylene: opaque panels are most effective, especially with interior lighting
• Mirror: reflects light, changes a room's perspective and gives you a chance to preen
• Fabric (see 47, 52): texture related to room's design; use in pleated or flat panels behind glass, wire, doweling, trellis or fretwork
• Painted mdf (see 73): easy to relate to a room's decoration and change and touch-up when necessary
• Wallpaper (see 76): use as built-in cupboard camouflage, either all over or as panels on the doors

# freestanding or built-in?

The classic arrangement of a freestanding wardrobe and chest of drawers is unlikely to satisfy modern clothes storage needs. Nowadays we all have so much stuff. Once you've worked out what it is you need to store, the next step is to decide if you want the sleekness of built-in furniture (sometimes with a hefty price tag) or the flexibility of freestanding.

## three freestanding options

1 • Self-assembly: at the economy end of the freestanding storage option, are perfectly adequate mdf self-assembly units with metal, mdf or softwood drawers, hanging rails and adjustable shelves fronted with sliding panels, doors or curtaining. Moving upmarket are systems that offer a greater variety of internal components and better finishes, for example, white lacquer, opaque glass or solid wood-framed doors and drawer fronts.

2 • Ready-made: more convenient, time-saving and stress-free, ready-assembled storage will probably be more strongly constructed.

3 • Antique: however handsome they look, an antique wardrobe or armoire is usually inadequately fitted inside for contemporary storage requirements, but you could get a joiner to adapt it for your needs. Check before you buy that the depth is adequate for a modern hanger.

### advantages
• No need to wait for delivery
• Flexible – easy to add to, adapt for changing needs or move around
• You can take it with you when you move

### disadvantages
• Less easy to create a co-ordinated look
• Less efficient use of space
• Less versatile interior space
• Limited range of materials

## room divider

One great use for freestanding furniture in a large bedroom or studio is the room divider comprising shelving and cupboard space. Buy an off-the-peg version or have one custom-built. It can either be static or fitted with sturdy, lockable wheels.

## two built-in options

1 • Off-the-peg: mass-produced fitted units are readily available, sometimes in units that can be linked together. The choices of finish are best suited to a modern urban interior and the best of these look sleek and unfussy.

2 • Made-to-order: offers the chance for storage that is completely in tune with your bedroom style and storage needs. Choose a carpenter whose work you have seen and like and who can help you make the most of the available space, for example those awkward-shaped places around the bed and en-suite fixtures. Think beyond standard finishes and details so your storage is as personal and different from the standard off-the-peg systems as possible.

## advantages

- Looks sleek and co-ordinated
- Efficient use of space
- Good selling point
- Can be purpose-built to suit a particular decorative style and to accommodate architectural elements such as a cornice and skirting boards
- Interior fittings can be purpose-built to suit personal requirements

## disadvantages

- Not for the impatient
- More costly than freestanding
- Lack of flexibility if your needs change
- Requires good DIY skills if self-assembly, otherwise, cost of professional installation
- You can't take it with you when you move

# 86 open shelves

Open shelves are versatile and should be chosen to blend with your bedroom's decor. You will need various sizes and widths to accommodate a mixture of items, but whatever their use, choose the same style throughout for a unified look. And as it's all too easy to overcrowd shelves you'll need to be rigorous in tidying them, otherwise the effect will be ruined.

## shelving to suit

Relate the style, size and construction of your shelving to your decorative scheme. Slim, floating shelves for a minimalist feel; ornate rococo style for the boudoir; bamboo and rope for the Zen interior.

## in proportion

It's important to 'balance' the look of the shelving to help the decorative flow. The best arrangement is in blocks, either vertical, pyramid-shaped or stepped. And try and position it near other furniture. In isolation on the wall shelving looks bulky.

## go with the flow

If you have fixed ceiling-to-floor shelving units, make sure their design continues the line of architectural features such as skirtings and cornices.

## let there be light

To add glamour to your shelving and reflect the light, 'line' the back of open shelves with mirror or alternatively edge them with a lip deep enough to conceal any downlights.

## storage as display

Use shelving to hold storage boxes made of wicker, rattan, bamboo, steel, fabric or the paper-covered variety. Chosen to complement your room style, these can be decorative in their own right.

## en suite

If you have a suitable window in your en suite, why not fix sturdy glass or mirrored shelves across it to hold toiletries, flowers and candles?

# 87

# clothes and shoes

In an ideal world, all our clothes and shoes would exactly fit into the allotted space in our bedroom in a miraculous and permanently tidy manner. Our ironing, folding and colour-coordinating skills would be supreme, and our rigorous annual review would ensure seamless seasonal changeovers. But in reality, we have to strive to create a workable clothes storage system, aided and abetted by some creative thinking and discipline!

## hanging clothes

Divide hanging space into sections for skirts, dresses, shirts and trousers according to length. This saves space. Item-specific hangers are very useful.

## folded clothes

Correctly folded garments take up less space. Chests of drawers or tallboys are one option for folded clothes, stacking boxes or baskets on wall-mounted brackets are others.

## shoes

Shoe racks, drawers, cubby holes and hanging holders will keep pairs of shoes united. Boots can be hung from clips on hangers or stuffed with boot trees. If you use hanging shoe bags, identify their contents with luggage labels and if shoe boxes are your thing, use a glued-on photo.

## socks and tights

Shoe bags and small laundry bags are great for storing socks and tights.

## belts and ties

If you don't mind having them on view, you could use an antique towel rail or a decorative ladder. Otherwise, hang them inside cupboard doors or on a hanging 'spinner'.

## scarves 'n' shawls

Pretty enough to be seen, you could make a feature of them by draping them over the back of a chair or hanging them from a table-top or floor-standing mirror.

## hats

Hats are awkward to store and take up a lot of space. The best solution are traditional hat boxes, covered in a pretty paper and left on view.

# by the bed

The sort of things you may want by your bed at night include a light, phone, alarm clock, books and magazines, notepad and pen, reading glasses, water and drinking glass, tissues, maybe flowers and a little photo or two – and those are just the things you see! How you deal with bedside storage will depend on how much room and stuff you have and the style of your bedroom.

## classic

A classic bedside table with a shelf underneath and a cupboard below is ideal. You can put the essentials on top, the often-needed on the shelf and the can't-shows in the cupboard!

## antique

Search antique shops or salerooms for an old nightstand with a cupboard that used to hold the pot. They look good in a traditional scheme and are practical too. Alternatively, you might find an ornate rococo-style side table or cupboard that would suit a boudoir look.

## off your trolley

A good solution to bedside storage, choose either a hospital style or a drinks trolley. It depends if your room has an industrial aesthetic or is in party mood!

## built-in

Some bed frames have integral tables, shelves or cupboards. They look streamlined but aren't very roomy.

## in the wall

A recessed shelf can be built into the wall behind the bed or even into a wide, purpose-built headboard. You could have downlights wired into it if you don't want wall-lights.

# space-savers

## doors and walls

There's often space above the door to include a cupboard and don't forget the wall above the bed. Back-of-door hooks and wall hooks are useful and you can fill corners with shelves or a cupboard.

## under the bed

A divan base or a contemporary design with drawers underneath (see 78) offers useful storage, as does a classic high bedstead (see 78) or a bed on a deep platform (see 32, 33).

## coat stand

A coat stand complete with good-looking hangers doesn't take up much room and is especially useful for guest rooms (see 35), while a fabric-draped frame with shelves and rails is the modern equivalent.

## windows and drawers

Build in a window seat or use the space for a deep ottoman and use drawer dividers to help you keep things neat and readily accessible.

# 90 solutions for small things

Small items like cosmetics, make-up, jewellery, loose change, buttons, pills, business cards, cuff-links, pens and sunglasses can be a real nuisance to keep safely stored yet readily accessible. Some of these receptacles will tame and contain them.

## boxes

In cardboard, wood, lacquer, leather, Perspex or metallic finish – choose a collection of one type to suit your bedroom style. And remember that hat boxes aren't just for hats. Cover them to suit – floral or toile paper for a girly boudoir, geometric abstracts for fifties retro – and leave them on show.

## baskets

Suiting a bedroom with a country or ethnic edge, woven baskets of all kinds add texture and convenience.

## bags

Stow small treasures and make-up in decorative handbags displayed on a shelf or pegs, or make small bags in a fabric to co-ordinate with your room.

## suitcases and hampers

Old leather and canvas cases or new metal ones are great for underwear, socks and toiletries in an urban loft-style or safari-look bedroom. Hampers are practical for the bedroom and the en suite for holding spare bedding, towels, light bulbs and toilet paper. Stack these in decreasing sizes to save room.

## bowls and pots

Glass, ceramic, wood, lacquer or wirework bowls or a row of terracotta, metal or ceramic flower pots can be used for make-up, change, jewellery and other odds and ends.

## mugs and glasses, cups and saucers

Colourful and decorative, use to hold small cosmetic items, pens and sunglasses. Pretty antique cups and saucers are inexpensive and are perfect for earrings, cuff links and loose change.

# help! what do I do with my entertainment centre?

Entertainment equipment has really come out of the closet. State-of-the-art technology has created audio and TV systems that are designed to be seen. But, however beautiful the system, you won't want to see a tangle of wires and leads so make sure they are well concealed. You obviously need the system to be in the best possible place for listening, viewing and operating (see 18) and, as we all know, size does matter in the bedroom so select a system whose size suits your space. If you feel that the whole thing interferes with your bedroom style, hide it behind a sliding screen or in a cupboard, or choose the smaller-is-less-of-an-eyeful option.

# finishing touches

Before turning to the fine detailing, which will stamp the bedroom with your personal style, there are still some practical questions to be answered and some decisions to be taken. For example, what will you use as a dressing table and where will you sit? Where will you perch to put your shoes on? Is a separate desk necessary? Will you want somewhere comfortable to feed your baby or read a book? Hopefully, if your answers mean you have to fit more furniture into the room, you'll have enough space to do so. Otherwise some creative thinking will be needed and that desk will have to double up as a make-up area, or that comfy chair will need to incorporate some useful storage.

# sitting and lounging

Most bedrooms need one practical chair. If you have room for a comfy chair, it's a bonus, while a sofa or chaise longue is a real luxury.

## essential seating

Choose a stylish, modern stool or a dainty cane or gilt chair to tuck under a dressing table. An upholstered ottoman also provides storage space.

Desk chairs come streamlined in pale wood or retro in stained, moulded plywood and metal. Alternatively, use a folding chair that you bring out when necessary.

## lounge lizard

Delicate upholstery fabric in the bedroom is usually acceptable because it's not subject to much wear and tear, but loose covers are often more practical. If you have the luxury of two sets you can rotate them seasonally.

Smart, sensuous and luxurious, a leather sofa or chair will outlive many styles and fashions. It can look clubby so you may want to soften its appearance with throws and cushions.

Chaises longues come in traditional or modern styles – velvet-covered and serpentine, or moulded shapes covered with leather or suede.

Canvas director's chairs or Perspex chairs are not usually associated with a bedroom, but they can work well. The non-colour and simple contours of Perspex allow it to mix with antique or modern ingredients. Lloyd Loom furniture is another bedroom option – but more for perching on than serious lounging.

You could also consider cane, wicker, rattan and bamboo, as well as planter's style chairs with their woven cane backs and seats. All these are light in style and will add a textural dimension. They are also versatile, mixing well with antique or modern furniture and with oriental or colonial bedrooms.

# tables and screens 94

A dressing table is an essential piece of bedroom furniture, especially if you don't have an en-suite bathroom, but you will need to have the luxury of space if you hope to include a writing table as well! If you're not meticulously tidy, a screen will help to hide a multitude of sins.

## five dressing table options

1 • Classic skirted kidney-shaped table for an opulent boudoir

2 • Rectangular with a 'tablecloth' top and skirt trimmed with crystal droplets

3 • Bevel-mirrored knee-hole table for an updated Art Deco bedroom

4 • Painted to suit

5 • Slim-profile console table

## writing table

It's best to keep a bedroom writing table small – unless, of course, your bedroom doubles as a study (see 34). A small one won't attract clutter or overwhelm the room. Look for the simplest design – slim-legged and narrow-topped in glass and steel, wood and paint or lacquer and inlay.

## screens

A screen provides privacy (see 63, 64), zones different areas of the room and even acts as a freestanding bedhead. It also adds an unusual vertical dimension.

• Indian, Moroccan, African or oriental fretwork are very decorative and allow some light to filter through.

• There are many well-finished contemporary designs in solid wood or you might find an old panelled screen. You could also have a screen made in timber, plywood or mdf.

• A shoji screen with opaque rice-paper panels makes an oriental-style division that is decorative and practical.

• A fabric-covered screen can echo your decorating scheme. For a tailored urban look go for an upholstered screen finished with braid or close nailing.

# mirrors

Mirrors reflect light, enhance the sense of space and are essential for dressing and toilette. In an en suite, mirror can be used on a large scale to make the often confined space less claustrophobic. Mirrors can also add another decorative element – bamboo framed for the oriental look, rococo curves for the French boudoir, geometric for Art Deco style, bevelled and etched for Venetian glamour.

## get dressed

A tall tilting mirror, or cheval glass, can stand anywhere convenient. There are reproduction antique styles or contemporary blond-wood-and-metal versions. A door-mounted mirror inside or outside a cupboard is practical if space is really tight while the latest casual chic looks favour a huge mirror in a carved frame simply propped on the floor against the wall.

## get made-up

Position a make-up mirror so the natural light shines on your face. You may also need artificial lighting on either side. A triple mirror gives a good view while a swivel mirror can be tilted to suit.

# picture perfect

A bedroom would be sterile without some pictures or decorative hangings. And remember, this is the room where you can indulge your taste without having to worry about what your visitors might think.

## balance and proportion

Using pictures in a group will make a greater decorative impact than dotting them around the room in a haphazard manner. A large piece of furniture makes a good 'anchor' for a group of pictures on the wall above, or a corner of the dressing table could be home to a gallery of small pictures. And if you have one large picture among small ones, put the large one at one end of the display.

There is something very soothing about a pair of symmetrically arranged pictures of equal size, perhaps one either side of the bed or window. But there are times when a single picture – one fabulous work of art above the bed – has more impact than a group. And if your bedroom's small, don't think that a large picture or piece of artwork is out of the question: it can look stunning in a small space.

You must also consider the colour of your walls. Pictures will have more 'weight' if they are hung

against a block of colour and the darker the colour, the more spectacular they will be. Heavily patterned wallpaper lessens the impact of pictures so if you also have a plain wall, hang the pictures there instead.

## frames and mounts

If you want impact, go for the heaviest, broadest frame you can find and a dramatic contrast between the style of the frame and the picture – for example, a battered antique gilded frame with a colourful modern painting.

Frame and mounts can unify a disparate collection of pictures. Using matching – but not necessarily the same sized – frames and mounts will bring a degree of harmony. Mounts can also be used to make small pictures look more impressive. But bear in mind as well that if a picture's beautiful enough, it won't necessarily require any frame or mount.

## to hang or not to hang?

Apart from the walls, where else can you display your pictures? A collection can be simply propped against a mantelpiece or even on the floor. Shelves offer another display space, or you might consider a single narrow, lipped shelf. This looks more interesting using pictures of various sizes and allowing some of them to overlap.

# objects and ornaments

However delightfully decorated, a bedroom that doesn't reflect your personality is a sad place indeed. This is where all those objects you've collected over the years come in. Edit them judiciously and you can't go wrong.

## the art of ornament

There is an art to display, so make your book collection more eye-catching in homemade paper covers in a single colour or limited range of colours. And group objects according to a common element: all wooden items, ceramics, and so on.

## arrangement matters

An arrangement on a wall has impact so choose tall, freestanding shelving units or shelving you can 'stack' into geometric shapes (see 86). Similarly, a large memo board with bits and pieces pinned on will have more impact than those same bits and pieces dotted around the room.

Finally, give large, single objects added night-time impact with an up- or downlight (see 56)

part three

# keeping it fresh

# what a refreshing experience! cleaning tips

It's so easy to let time go by without a thorough spring-cleaning, but it can be cathartic and will make a lot of difference to the presentation of your bedroom, so get that duster out.

## mattress

A mattress should be turned twice a year. Don't vacuum it because that draws particles of skin and dust-mite faeces to the surface.

## bed dressing

If you have any sort of bed drapes, dust will inevitably collect in the folds. If possible, wash them once a year, otherwise dry-clean or vacuum in situ, then take them down and shake them outside.

## on the floor

Once a year, make sure you have carpets and rugs professionally cleaned. They will not only look better but will last longer too. If you have a hard floor, follow the manufacturer's advice for cleaning.

## hidden horrors

It's amazing what you find when you look into and under things: dust has a way of getting everywhere, so pull out drawers and completely empty your wardrobes. And move the bed too. Apart from making cleaning easier, you might just find that missing earring or shoe.

## sweetly scented

When you have your annual or bi-annual clear-out, take the opportunity to keep your clothes smelling good with scented hanging sachets, and moth-free with pleasant-smelling cedarwood balls. Drawers can be refreshed with fragrant lining paper and scented sachets or soaps distributed among clothes, underwear and towels.

# make it over

When your bedroom starts looking a little tired but you're not ready for a complete change, making a few minor adjustments will add new zest.

## giving curtains an edge

Because curtain styles can have such a profound effect on the look of a room, any changes you make to them will have instant impact. Try adding a deep contrast-coloured border or sewing on an unusual decorative trim along the front edge when you fancy a change.

## changing seasons

A seasonal change of curtains provides both a refreshingly alternative look and an opportunity to have curtains cleaned or repaired. And you could keep different sets of bedding to harmonise with the change in curtains – dark colours and heavy textures for winter, light neutral cottons and linens for summer.

## cushions

Cushion covers are easy and inexpensive to make, so you can ring the changes, perhaps with different seasonal looks as you do for curtains and bedding. Some new shapes will make all the difference, too.

## loose and lovely

Loose covers aren't just for sofas: they work perfectly well for small, easy chairs too. Or envelope covers held in place with fabric ties are an easy-to-make alternative.

## get a handle on it

Something as simple as changing the handles will update a tired chest of drawers or cupboard. There are many smart or amusing designs to suit any bedroom scheme.

## a lick of paint

Changing the colour of a single wall will re-focus your bedroom style dramatically. If you picked the original colour from a patterned fabric used in the room, choose a different colour this time round. And if your bedroom doesn't have much pattern in it, you could add some coloured stripes, circles or squares while you're at it. Similarly, a coat or two of paint will transform tired old furniture or cupboards.

## exchange is no robbery

If a piece of furniture isn't fulfilling its function, doesn't really suit the look of the room or you've simply grown tired of it, then perhaps it should be banished or exchanged for something more serviceable and decorative.

# 100

## flowers and plants

Flowers appeal to us with their beauty and sentimental associations, but, above all, their scent is vital for a soothing bedroom environment.

### take your pick

Bedroom flowers don't need to make a complex decorative statement. You can just use them in tiny, intimate arrangements for the bedside or dressing table, or try a scented flower head floating in a broad, flat bowl of water. It will perfume and re-hydrate your bedroom at the same time. A single highly perfumed lily or delicate orchid would be a good choice for the en suite, which is often florally neglected, and remember that flowers can be used as a subtle means of echoing or contrasting with colour accents in the bedroom.

### seasons

Flowers are the natural witness to the seasons and there is a particular pleasure in choosing plants and flowers that genuinely reflect the time of year. Particularly in an urban environment, it's easy to lose sight of what's in flower, so reconnect with nature and choose your bedroom flowers with the season in mind.

### avoiding allergies

There's an old tradition that flowers should be removed from the bedroom at night because they were considered unhealthy. Better to remove the pollen-bearing stamens where necessary to prevent allergic reactions and, where lilies are concerned, to prevent pollen stains.

### flowers and herbs for aromatherapy

Aromas that comfort the mind and body are especially suitable for the bedroom. Think lavender, camomile, rosemary and bergamot. Crush their leaves lightly to release the aromatic oils into the air.

Alternatively you might prefer pillows stuffed with dried flowers – the most popular are lavender – or essential-oil burners. Just don't leave them burning all night.

### traditional flowers

Roses are a classic choice for a traditional bedroom, but only choose those that are rich in fragrance, rather than the perfect-bud but no-scent florist's alternatives!

### modern flowers

For a minimalist bedroom try an orchid or a single branch of cherry blossom in a spectacular container, perhaps placed in front of the window where the natural light will accentuate the shape, or lit from beneath against a textural or coloured backdrop.

# 101

## a change is as good as a rest

# index

# acknowledgements

## Author's acknowledgements

To Jane O'Shea, thank you for giving me the opportunity to write this book. To Hilary Mandleberg, warmest gratitude for her endlessly good-natured guidance. To Paul Welti, thanks and admiration for his book layout. Finally, huge love to my husband, Francis, for patience, encouragement and emergency cooking.